MAKING GROUPS

Making groups work: rethinking practice

Joan Benjamin, Judith Bessant and Rob Watts

ALLEN & UNWIN

First published in 1997 by
Allen & Unwin
9 Atchison Street
St Leonards NSW 2065
Australia
Phone: (61 2) 9901 4088
Fax: (61 2) 9906 2218
E-mail: frontdesk@allen-unwin.com.au
URL: http://www.allen-unwin.com.au

National Libarary of Australia
Cataloguing-in-Publication entry:

Benjamin, Joan.
    Making groups work: rethinking practice.

    Bibliography.
    Includes index.
    ISBN 1 86448 304 0.

    1. Social groups. 2. Work groups. I. Bessant, Judith.
    II. Watts, Rob. III. Title.

305

Set in 10/12 Times by DOCUPRO, Sydney

Printed by SRM Production Services Sdn Bhd, Malaysia

10 9 8 7 6 5 4 3 2 1

Contents

Acknowledgments

There are many people who have helped with this project and we would like to thank them. Lenny Jenner and his work with a group of people with disabilities are doing important work. We are privileged to be able to present some of their work. Colin Benjamin provided invaluable assistance and support when we needed it most. Dr Ruth Webber and Dr Bob Bessant have offered their time and expertise as readers and have provided us with valuable feedback for which we are most grateful. We would also like to thank Elery Hamilton-Smith and Roger Trowbridge for their willingness to offer advice and information on the development of modern group work. We also thank artist Judith Cameron for her contribution to the front cover of this book.

The Department of Sociology, Social Welfare and Administration at the Australian Catholic University provided a collegial culture that is strongly supportive of research and for this Judith Bessant is most appreciative. The Department of Social Sciences at RMIT supported Rob Watts in the writing of this book. Many of our students have collaborated with us in developing our understanding of groups and communities over the years and we especially appreciate the contribution of the Youth Affair students at RMIT.

Joan Benjamin
Judith Bessant
Rob Watts

Part I

Introduction

Introduction: Setting the agenda for groups and group work

Introduction

It is stating the obvious to observe that all of us spend most of our lives living and working in groups. In the twentieth century, sociologists and psychologists have been fascinated by the fact that being human means being part of groups like families, schools and clubs. But this was known long before academics 'discovered' groups. As Samuel Johnson, the eighteenth century English writer, put it, 'In civilised society, we all depend upon each other.'

Paradoxically, our social landscape has been shaped by the ideas and prejudices of Western liberalism and the belief that we are all 'individuals'. Despite living and working in groups, some of us may like to think we are self-reliant and separate from 'society'—much like Robinson Crusoe, the hero of Defoe's novel about a sailor lost on a desert island who invents a one-man society before he is rescued. Despite such fantasies, the truth is that we spend a lot of time in an ocean of people and groups.

Some of these groups are large and others are small; some are complex and others are simple; some are groups that meet only once, while others may last for decades. Some groups are central to our experiences of becoming a person—there are certain groups that we interact with from the moment of our birth. This is especially true of that primal group we call 'the family', although there are many kinds of family. Other important groups where we spend a lot of time include early play and kindergarten groups or school-based groups. Other groups are optional, but provide us with a context in which to learn particular skills or ways of relating to people. Such groups include scouts or guides, or the karate or the netball club we go to after school or work. We join some groups to provide a change of environment. Women who work all day in the home may join a parents and teachers group or form a play group to provide them with some support, as well as enabling them to get out of the house and meet other people. Some men take refuge in groups at the local pub or the TAB, while others are members of groups made up of fellow workers in a trade union or professional association, or formed to raise funds for charity. Some of us join political parties and/or become involved in various forms of social action or social movements because we feel strongly about certain issues and want them solved. There are also more fluid groups of friends and relatives who we meet over drinks or dinners or at special occasions like weddings, Christmas or funerals.

Some of us join long-standing groups like the Young Women's Christian Association (YWCA) or the Australian Women's National League. Some of us also belong to groups that are historical and have a sense of tradition like the Masons. These are often large organisations with a vigorous 'group-think' culture which set out to influence their members overtly. Think of organisations like the army, various religious orders, or groups like nurses or the police.

We are not always able to decide whether or not we will become a member of a particular group. Quite often, this 'just happens' and we have no choice. We are born into some groups. Sometimes we join them unwittingly and occasionally absent-mindedly, or we can join them happily and sometimes leave them angrily. But whatever we do, most of us belong to groups of some kind; we live within them and experience quite different types of relationships and emotions inside them. What we experience in groups is important, especially for the people who have set them up or who join them with a purpose in mind, or who intend to work with groups and use them to achieve certain aims. This is where group work comes in.

Why we have written this book

We have used the shorthand phrase 'group work' to mean 'working *with* groups' and 'working *in* groups', rather than referring to a particular technique for or approach to '*doing* group work'. This book has several motives behind it.

First, we believe group work is important because working with people in groups has many advantages:

- Groups provide opportunities to share experiences, develop and pursue common aims, learn from each other and receive support from each other.
- Groups offer the chance to sort out relationship issues or political differences as well as the chance to develop and try out new skills.
- Sometimes groups help to reduce social isolation and loneliness by increasing opportunities to meet new people.
- Groups can be powerful sources of social change, which can help members challenge sexual or racial stereotypes. They can provide new role models and resources to overcome social exploitation or political oppression.
- Groups can also be major arenas for developing new political and social movements.
- Groups can help people to link their personal identity with larger social movements. For instance, they can help women integrate being feminists with the day-to-day business of working or being part of a family (see Toseland & Rivas 1984, pp. 8–9).

While believing that working in groups and understanding how groups work is important, we have been concerned about two aspects of introductory group work textbooks used in Australian universities, TAFE colleges, neighbourhood houses and community agencies: there is widespread reliance on overseas group work texts, and most group work texts used in Australia are too abstract in nature.

To address the first issue, it is important that we start to write Australian books for Australian audiences. The books used in Australia are predominantly written by British or North American writers drawing on British or North American experiences and situations to make their points. Most of the reading guides used in Australian universities and TAFE colleges are dominated by British and American texts like Sprott (1958), Rogers (1969), Milson (1973), Blumberg & Golembiewski (1976), Button (1972, 1974, 1982a, 1982b) and Douglas (1976, 1979, 1983).

There is also a vast psychological and sociological research literature on groups that lies in the background and supports such books. We are uncomfortable with the assumption that anything that comes from overseas must be better, more authoritative or more credible than any local product. Much of Australia's history has operated on the assumption (found in all colonial societies) that

'Home' was somewhere else where 'real' ideas and 'great' music and painting and culture were produced. This 'cultural cringe' is still alive and well in Australia and needs to be challenged. Linked to this is the assumption that ideas, theories or practices can be transplanted from one place (say, England in the 1970s) to another (Australia in the 1990s) because local context and knowledge are irrelevant.

This is the first critical, contemporary and commercially published general book on group work that has been written by Australian authors for Australian human service professionals and practitioners, teachers of group work, students and community activists. However, a small and valuable body of Australian books dealing with groups does exist. Some of these are now hard to find because they have been out of print for some time—for example, the very valuable compilation of 'structured experiences' for group work by Watson et al. (1980). Other works include specialist books which have been around for a long time, such as Gale (1974), and the more recent general group work text by Tyson (1989), designed primarily as a tool for management and organisational development. Tyson's book sits firmly in what we call the 'abstracted' style. Other works take a specialist look at one aspect of group work, such as the fine treatment of the use of psycho-drama techniques in group work in Williams (1991).

In the main, the few Australian writers who have written on group work, like the international writers, have not written about group work in a way that recognises the social complexity of groups and the people who comprise them. The exceptions include Duke & Sommerlad (1981) and Szirom & Dyson (1984). Duke & Sommerlad have drawn attention to the ways the interest in personal growth and change which characterises some group work can take place at the expense of an interest in social and political change. Szirom & Dyson offer a highly specified feminist group work model for women-only groups.

It is important in group work to remember the social context and political purpose of groups. The second major problem we have with most of the group work books used in Australia is their abstracted quality. Rarely does the reader have a sense that the author is writing about real people in real groups in real settings. Nor have many of these writers dealt with the fact that group work is a highly political process.

The tendency has been to bury the complexity and qualities of our lives in groups under the weight of 'theory' and abstracted writing. Many authors seem hesitant to produce 'objective' accounts of groups. Look at the way some of the standard textbooks answer the question 'what is a group?'.

A group is:

- . . . a dynamic social entity composed of two or more individuals, interacting independently in relation to one or more common goals that are valued by its members, so that each member influences and is influenced by each other member, to some degree, through face to face communication. Over time, if the individuals who comprise the group continue to assemble, they tend to develop means for determining who is and who is not a member, statuses and roles for members, and values and norms that regulate behaviour of consequence to the group. (Bertcher 1979, p. 14)
- Two or more persons who are interacting with one another in such a manner that each person influences and is influenced by each other person. (Shaw 1981, p. 8)
- . . . a small, face-to-face collection of persons who interact to accomplish some purpose. The group will meet for one or more sessions, have *open ended membership* (where people come and go as they see fit) or *closed membership* (where people are constrained to attend for a specified time) and are either *time limited* (with the time in hours and the number of meetings usually specified) or *time unlimited* (without a definite ending time or date). (Brown 1991, pp. 3–4)
- . . . a plurality of individuals who are in contact with one another, who take one another into account, and who are aware of some significant commonality. An essential feature of a group is that its members have something in common and that they believe that what they have in common makes a difference. (Zastrow 1989, p. 7)

A comment

Those who offer clear and sharp definitions about people and social behaviour seem reluctant to acknowledge the overwhelming complexity of human existence. Establishing authoritative definition/s involves approaching all the big issues and questions about who we are and why we do what we do. Defining people or processes can be like putting living beings into boxes. However, given the limitations of rigid definitions, they do also have some value in that they provide a basis for some agreement on what we are talking about when we refer to a 'group'.

We all know what a group is, despite their actual diversity, so there does not seem to be much point trying to define a group—even if such an 'essential' definition were possible or even useful.

Some writers talk about 'the group' or 'groups' as if they were not made up of real people with actual differences between them. Thus we get Australian writers like O'Connor et al. (1995, p. 134) stating that:

> A group, like a network, may be defined as a system of relationships between and among people. The group has structure, social cohesion, goals and accepted ways of doing business.

The first sentence does not say anything that we do not already 'know', while the second sentence confuses prescription with description.

One of the modern doyens of group work, Douglas (1983, p. 3), writes that all human groups share certain universal characteristics:

> The similarities of all human groupings can be shown to reside in an identifiable number of variables that are ubiquitously present, but in differing intensity and importance whenever human beings are gathered together.

Douglas believes that human groups are similar because the variables that allegedly make them similar are present whenever groups of people get together. Douglas (1983, p. 171) explains how a group keeps itself together:

> Membership of a group is maintained by continued production of acceptable behaviour. This must equally involve rejecting the temptation to non-conforming behaviour and so too the rejection of ideas and beliefs that are contrary to, or even just different from, those held by the group in general.

Our response is that what Douglas claims is *sometimes* true; however, it is possible to belong to a group for many years and for that group to be full of tempestuous difficulties, different viewpoints and violent antipathies. Similarly, many women remain in violent and abusive families and marriages for years. This definition fails to address issues of gender, for example. This also points to the conspicuous absence of questions of power and gender in so much of the existing group work literature. Exceptions like Szirom & Dyson (1984) test this rule; using some of the principles of group work, these Australian authors have developed a good feminist manual of exercises and approaches designed to promote personal skills like assertiveness for young women in all-women group settings.

Further, much of the literature produced about group work is conservative and restricted both politically and ethically. Few of the texts, for example, refer to the possible use of group work by progressive or radical social movements, or discuss the work of people like Saul Alinsky or Paulo Friere, who have used groups to promote quite progressive social change. Much of the writing about group work is also abstracted and often incorrect. There is no reason to assume for example, that groups have to be 'small', or that groups have to operate with a totalitarian insistence on consensus, or that everyone 'influences' everyone else.

We live and work in a variety of institutions and organisations. Institutions include relationships like families, households and friendships. As our century winds down, more of us can be found in organisations. Organisations include capitalist companies like BHP, clubs like the RSL, associations like the YMCA or complex bureaucratic places like universities, government departments, big insurance companies and schools. Organisations come in all sizes, but they can all be viewed as a system of small groups.

As human beings, we associate with other people in informal as well as formal ways. Think how often we refer to 'in-groups' and 'out-groups', 'outsiders' and 'insiders', 'us' and 'them', and 'factions' and 'cliques'. Each one of these terms indicates the presence of groups.

We have all worked in groups where love and friendship reigned most of the time, and we have worked in other groups where the members have despised or hated each other. Many groups include people who don't like the group, its purpose or its existence and who will say so if given half a chance. Some groups work well with a lot of consensus and others work well without much consensus. We have worked in groups where we got to know a lot about everyone else—sometimes perhaps too much—and we have been in other groups where we got to be known to only a few people. Undoubtedly, groups that are going to produce some results for some of the people some of the time will have a sense of a minimum common purpose and their members will be able to talk to each other enough to make themselves understood.

Most of the proponents of mainstream group work—found, for example, in youth work, where it is touted as *the* skill that distinguishes youth workers from other 'helping professions'—tend to regard group work and the use of structured experiences—for example, playing various games (from 'Icebreaker' through 'Lifeboat' to 'Hollow Square') in groups—as ends in themselves. Button (1974, p. 13) defends the use of structured experiences in his version of 'developmental group work' thus:

> [Developmental group work is] a way of offering people opportunities for vital experiences with other people, through the membership of supportive groups who are learning to help one another in personal ways. It is developmental and educative as distinct from problem or crisis based. Our ambition is to help young people to build up their personal resources so that they can cope more adequately with life and its problems as it comes along.

There is no reflection here on the fact that these structured experiences are taking place in institutional settings like schools and universities, where young people are compelled to spend more and more time. Many of the young people we refer to are dependent, subject to unremitting adult scrutiny, supervision and endless rhetoric about how they are being 'empowered' in educational institutions where they spend a considerable amount of time playing games with people who are often poorly equipped to facilitate the group process (Cooper & White 1994). The impact of stripping more and more young people away from the streets, workplaces and household sites where the opportunity to deal with real issues and problems was traditionally experienced, needs to be better understood and dealt with. In this context, structured experiences in group work classes represent a false exercise in simulating life issues which young people are being economically and socially compelled to forego.

So much modern group work has this enclosed, introverted quality, in which false games are used to try to simulate life. Too much group work is about using structured experiences or games for training people for prescribed stages in the life cycle (for example, Forming, Storming, Norming, Performing and Mourning), rather than getting on with important issues and solving important problems associated with our society's unprecedented social, political, moral and economic change.

This would not have pleased some of the great figures in the international history of group work, like Kurt Lewin. Lewin (1890–1947) made no secret of the fact that his own 'scientific' study of groups, and his development of those experiential learning techniques that have become so common a part of group work education, was directly linked to the struggle against anti-democratic tendencies like Nazism in the 1940s and 'communism' in the Cold War after 1945. As Lewin (1943, p. 126) put it during the Second World War, 'There is no hope for creating a better world without a deeper scientific insight into the function of leadership and culture and other essentials of group life'.

Sometimes the politics of group work are not so simple. But the political character of group work is inescapable, as we make clear throughout this book. By 'political' here, we refer to fundamental questions about the moral choices all of us have to make. These issues include basic questions like: Whose side are you on? What do you mean by social justice? Is this a good thing to do or to say? Good group work is able to address these kinds of questions. It is simply not possible to escape or evade the political issues that group work, like any other form of social intervention, inevitably raises. We think a long overdue feature of this book is the way we spell out our preferred political position as we outline the issues and approaches to group work we think are important.

Finally, we think it is vital that we stop assuming that group work only refers to groups run by professionals, or to group work undertaken in professional workplaces. Being in groups is a basic feature of social existence. All of us use groups and live in them and one of our hopes is that, by adopting a more expanded view of groups and group work, we can help people to work in groups more effectively.

Why this book is different

Our book sets out to be different in a number of ways. First, we want to integrate the critical perspective offered in the first half of the book with some of the more 'applied', 'how-to' material presented in the second half of the book. We believe people who work in the human services need to be able to develop a thoughtful and critical approach to what they do. At the same time, it is important that we are able to act effectively. Even though he often failed to follow his own advice, Karl Marx put the point well when he said

in the 1840s that it was not enough merely to interpret the world—
'the point is to change it'.

Second, we want to focus specifically on some of the experiences
of Australians who work in and with groups. We want to restore
theory to what it used to mean before the positivists got their hands
on it and turned it into a series of high-level generalisations, or
'laws' based on scientific data-gathering. We want theory to mean
the practice of reflecting on our experience, of making sense of
things we do or have done, and communicating this to others.

Third, we want this book to reflect the fact that groups cannot
be discussed as if they were essentially always the same everywhere,
or as if they were subject to the same dynamics or factors irrespective of their membership. We thus emphasise the role of difference
in groups and in our identities.

One of the more interesting shifts in social science, and especially
in sociology and cultural studies, over the last two decades has been
the focus given to issues of *identity* and *difference* (Giddens 1991).
Once sociologists and social psychologists used to tell a simple story
about how something called 'society' produced 'roles' (like 'man'
or 'woman', 'teacher' or 'criminal'). *Roles* were a set of rules and
values and aspirations for living as a member of a *society*. *Socialisation* was the mechanism by which new members of that 'society'
were poured into their appropriate roles. As Wrong argued (1969),
it was a story which drew on the metaphor of the factory assembly
line in which people were treated as plastic material poured into
moulds, with 'society' being the 'factory'. Sometimes something
went wrong with the moulding process and deviants were produced.
But mostly the assembly line worked and something called 'social
order' was the outcome.

It was never a particularly good story, but social scientists were
wedded to a view of their work as a proper science. They thought
they could study the way people behaved as if they were just like
chemicals or atoms. People were apparently forced to behave by
larger 'structures' (like 'society') and 'causes'. This approach failed
to deal with the obvious mess of ordinary social experience or with
the fact that real people kept producing social change and disorder.
It also failed to deal with the problem of identity. The grand
theoretical work (associated with the likes of Parsons, Merton or
Coleman) implied that identity was a simple *and* uncomplex thing.

However, real people experienced these social roles in ways that
were unlike the simple, neat, uncomplicated explanations offered by
sociological theory. The rash of new social movements that began

in the 1960s, like the black civil rights movement, the women's movement (or feminism) and the gay and lesbian movements began to tell different stories. In particular, the question of identity became more fluid, and was often a contradictory experience (Aronowitz 1988). Modern social theory is now trying to make sense of this question of identity (Beck et al. 1994). The relationship between group work and identity is one of the themes we explore in this book.

Identity deals with the fact that our 'self' is an inside–outside business. Our identity is something we experience both from the 'inside' in terms of our feelings and thinking, as well as being something other people deal with from the 'outside' when they talk to us, or shake our hands or yell at us. In the course of all our daily interactions with other people, an elaborate ongoing dialogue is happening between our inside and our outside experiences. This also means we have to deal with the ways *other* people relate to *us* from the 'outside'. People experience themselves from the inside and outside in different ways. Skin colour, age, body shape, the way we talk, our sexuality and the way we dress all reveal something about our 'inside' *and* shape the way the 'outside' deals with each of our 'selves'.

Men and women share some things but they *are* different; they think, feel and interact in ways that are different. Freud observed many years ago that the first thing you notice about a person you meet for the first time is their sex, whether they are male or female. Yet, as important as gender is in shaping a particular person's sense of self and their identity, it is only one element. As Connell (1995) argues, what it means to be a man or a woman varies not only in different places and times, but can even be different for people in the same place and time depending on who they are with and what they are doing. As Connell puts it, our identity as a 'man' or as a 'woman' is 'a precarious achievement'. Other things go into making *identity* and *difference*. Koori men and Nyungar women are different from Lebanese men and Greek women. Middle-class professional heterosexual Anglo-Celtic men do things differently from young Italian lesbian women. It is surely time to incorporate these simple observations into how we think about group work, and how we do it.

You will not find simple or uncomplicated formulae for working with something called 'groups' in this book. There is no such thing as 'the group' or any one thing called 'group work'. Instead, there are groups made up of people who may be very different from other kinds of people. And, of course, there are different kinds of group facilitators, different contexts and different aims and objectives.

What is group work?

As in many other professions and occupations, there are many rivalries and jealousies in the human services. Conflict between social workers and youth workers, community development workers and school teachers, housing workers and feminist paramedics, community nurses, environmentalists and credit counsellors frequently erupts when one or more of these groups claims another group of workers 'do not know what they're doing' or 'are not doing anything useful', and 'anyway they're using a technique like group work which is really "our" technique and/or they do not know how to use it properly'. We cannot possibly hope to overcome such conflicts with a single textbook, but it is worth reflecting on what is really at stake here.

To add to these complexities, there are no neat, simple, uncomplicated definitions of 'group work' or of 'working with groups'. It is true that group workers set up groups of people with a degree of deliberateness. Group work can refer, then, to the kinds of groups some of us deliberately set up and to the kinds of activities we perform to achieve a wide range of aims and objectives. But group work also happens when people get together to try to solve a problem or engage in some kind of change. Working with groups is not a single technique or methodology. It refers to a vast array of activities designed to be used for a multitude of purposes with a wide range of particular people in mind. It can encompass everything from group therapy and social group work to groups set up to achieve consciousness-raising, self-help or even forms of overt political and community action.

Group workers are people who use groups and who often lead or manage groups to achieve a range of outcomes. Often group facilitators put a lot of effort into identifying and developing ideas, rules and values for the members of the group. This aids in clarifying the purpose of the group, to help members work out *why* they are in the group. It is true that most groups, so long as they stay intact, have some basis in the common sense of purpose of their members. Groups often exist despite all the members disagreeing violently about lots of things, because they share enough to want to keep the group going.

Our kind of group work

This book does not deal with every kind of group or every kind of group work technique; rather, it covers several different forms of group work. Whilst it is aimed at different styles of group workers or facilitators in Australia, it does not encompass all the kinds of group work undertaken in Australia. One focus is on group work done with young people. Another is on the styles of group work which aim to produce changes in social relations and which promote social action. Group work can take place for any number of reasons and engage all sorts of people. We bring to this our own political and ethical preferences and assumptions, which we have written about as clearly as possible.

What is in the book?

The introduction, which begins Part I, has set the agenda, outlining the core themes of the book: the diversity of perspectives in group work; the need to be thoughtful and explicit about our political objectives; and the role played by groups in promoting agency.

Chapter 1 examines aspects of the use of small-group techniques by one group worker in a group of people with disabilities. For these people with physical disabilities, the experience of working in a group is all about the use of stories to recapture a sense of identity.

Part II, 'Perspectives', introduces the reader to the differences that characterise modern group work. In Chapters 2, 3 and 4 we pose a central question: what is group work? It is answered by asking why and how people have undertaken group work. We turn to the history of group work and to contemporary group work practice for guidance. We begin by looking at the origins of group work in a whole variety of experiments and styles of intervention, many of them beginning in the nineteenth century. We look at the history of group work, its use in therapy and the use made of it for social control. Then we look at three different perspectives and the ways these perspectives are found in some five different kinds of group work. The contemporary practice of group work reveals various commitments to social control, self-help, empowerment and social change. We survey (very quickly) the ways in which group work is found in all sorts of organisations, including scouting and feminist groups, sporting groups, business groups, public-sector personnel practices and the like. Many different purposes and interests have been associated with group work throughout its history, including social control, therapy and remedial interventions.

The three chapters in Part III, 'Doing It', look at some of the practice issues involved in working with groups. Our stress is very much on working in and with groups and using those approaches to group work that enhance people's sense of *agency*. In this way, while what we say looks like a 'nuts and bolts' approach, we believe it carries the general points made in the critical perspectives set up in the first two parts of the book about the need to promote agency, pursue democracy and be thoughtful and clear about one's political commitments. In Chapter 5 we look at what might be called the life-cycle of groups, examining such things as the stages in groups and how group workers can learn to 'read' the life-stages of groups as well as developing facilitation skills. In Chapter 6 we begin to systematically explore the purposes of group work, beginning with a commitment to collaborative learning, and stress an active and critical approach to using structured experiences in groups. Chapter 7 offers a cluster of structured experiences for use by students and others to illustrate the points made in this book. In Chapter 8, we look at the role of group work in promoting a variety of forms of social change and community development.

Who is this book for?

The book is designed to be read and used by a variety of people, including people who are working in neighbourhood houses, students in schools, tertiary and further education (TAFE) colleges and university human service courses in areas like youth work, community development and social work; it is intended for use by teachers and academic staff, by people who train others in group work and by practitioners.

The text in each chapter is followed by a set of Review Questions. Finally, a short but useful Glossary on pp. 189–91 defines some of the key concepts in this field.

1

Group work in Australia:
The question of agency

> In a group run on action lines, members find a strange voice, which they may begin to recognise as their own; they feel the gush of their life building up . . . Is *this* who I am? They tell stories about themselves in terms of their personal or work related problems.
>
> *(Williams 1991, p. 1)*

In this chapter we lay the foundations of some of the themes discussed in later chapters. Most of the chapter consists of a story told by an able-bodied person who is working with a group of people who have some disabilities. This story contains some crucial ideas. First, the experience of this particular group of people with disabilities provides an insight into the value of exploring our place in groups and our use of them—which is related to the idea of *identity*. Second, it provides an opportunity to look at the role of *stories* in understanding our identity. Finally, we suggest that 'doing' group work, or working with groups, can involve everything from telling stories to planning for social change and each has a place in pursuing what we refer to as *agency*. Each of these themes is central to modern group work.

From 'disability' to agency: Telling stories and contemporary group work

Most of us live and work in large cities, which can often be cold, anonymous, professionalised environments. The city is a world busy with the ant-like activities of thousands of professional workers such as teachers, social workers, doctors and bureaucrats who help run the state and its hive of welfare, education and health care institutions. In such a world, many of us turn to friends and families for a little warmth. In one Australian city (Melbourne), a small group of people with a lot of experience of that world began to make their own history, much of it focused on telling stories about the problems they had experienced in being able to have friends.

Throughout 1994 and 1995, a small group of men and women (Arthur, Claire, David, Ian, Jenny, Melinda and Sue) met with a Melbourne-based academic and group worker, Lenny Jenner. They met in pubs, motels and houses. The group was not an 'ordinary' group, since most members had a range of physical disabilities—some of them quite serious. Some had very little control over their physical movements and many could not speak easily or clearly; some shook a lot or did not always have as much control over parts of their bodies as others; most used various machines with which to communicate; some spent a lot of time using pointers to type out sentences to communicate. All members of this group were used to being identified by other, often more powerful, people as 'disabled'.

Lenny was involved in the group as an 'able-bodied' person. He was interested in finding out how the identities of people with disabilities could be affected by membership of a group which was exploring, revealing and redefining the experiences of disability, identity and friendship in a context shaped by the stories of 'normalism' (Fulcher 1989).

'Normalism'

'Normalism' has to do with the fact that all of us have differences in a world where we all want to be 'normal'. Remember that *all of us* have and do things that make us different. Some of us are 'short' (or 'tall') or have black hair (or red hair) or bits of our bodies are missing (like foreskins, legs or fingers), or we have different kinds of skin colour or shapes of eyes or noses. Some of us go to school for long periods of time and some of us leave early. The list of differences is endless and infinite. Difference is everywhere. But difference is not the same thing as inequality. Regrettably, some of 'us' use certain differences that can be seen on any street in any Australian city to infer that some of us are really 'other' people who are in some way very different, abnormal and unequal.

One way of converting 'difference' into 'inequality' is to name people in particular ways. This happens particularly when those names are put into stories about how the 'other' group of people is said to be more stupid, dependent, lazier, more drunk, less intelligent, more promiscuous and so on. The categories used to name certain people are usually the result of concepts that are imposed by other people.

In the case of the group of people discussed here, the very words used to name them (like 'disabled people') were not devised by those to whom the concept or category was applied. Furthermore, these names have a central place in stories that have been used to tell about the 'other' groups and those doing the telling have traditionally been in dominant, powerful positions of authority. Furthermore, it has been that authority, or the power of those doing the naming, that has given credibility and truth status to stories told about the people to whom these categories were applied. These are stories about 'normalism' (Corbett 1994).

Part of the experience of being marginalised and dominated also has to do with the way some of 'us' call 'others' (Abberley 1987). One way to dominate and exclude a person or group of people from institutions like work, school, health care or the law courts, or from relationships of mutual trust or esteem, is to insist that the differences that all of us manifest can be grouped and then used to indicate that some of us are not really properly human, or are not 'moral', or have no right to be respected.

Our identity is revealed in stories and understood via narrative. Using these stories, we want to reflect on how group experiences help shape identity. As discussed later in the book, groups are ideal places for telling our stories, whether we be someone with a special history or whether our story is about being a woman, or gay, or a Lebanese worker, or whatever.

'Normalism' has a history that still has to be fully told. Writers like Canguilhem (1993), Foucault (1979), Rose (1989) and Lewis (1987) have begun to pave the way in the telling of those stories. They have been particularly widespread in places like schools, hospitals, asylums and prisons since the early nineteenth century. And they have been told by groups of professionals—especially doctors, psychologists and teachers. The work of many professionals has been directed towards measuring the incidence of 'normality' in relation to factors such as intelligence, nutrition and physical fitness among the general population, thereby setting the standards against which those who were not 'normal', or not average, could be discovered, diagnosed and then cared for.

Many of these scientific and caring activities were tied to bigger, national stories about the government's need to know about the health and wellbeing of the whole population. Such information was important because governments had been engaged in international struggles over ideology, empire and trade and therefore needed to be able to call on all of their resources should war or conflict erupt. States also needed to know about the condition of their human resources to establish what used to be called 'national efficiency and hygiene' (Rose 1989). Until the middle of the twentieth century, many people who were deemed not to be 'normal' physically or intellectually were measured, identified, diagnosed, managed, institutionalised, sterilised, placed in sheltered workshops or special schools, locked up, medicated or even sometimes murdered in campaigns of eugenics designed to improve the fitness and strength of the entire population. Much of this interest in the disabled was aroused by compassion. However, as Nietszche reminded us, compassion can sometimes take on a dangerous—even murderous—quality.

From this longstanding definition of disability, and the myriad of institutions, professions and organisations established to 'help' the 'disabled', emerged a movement by people with disabilities whose aim was to reclaim their identity. The group work process described here is one small expression of this, offering insights into the ways in which group processes can intersect with issues of identity (Jenner 1995). It becomes clear that this group process embodied a number of different purposes and goals. Lenny Jenner's research was designed, amongst other things, to get him a Master's degree; this ran alongside members' desire to learn from the group experience with the objective of achieving a growing capacity for *agency*. The story that follows is told by Lenny Jenner and emphasises the central role played in our collective lives by story telling.

Background to the group work experience (as told by Lenny Jenner)

From the 1970s, workers in the Spastic Society, particularly those in areas of recreation, accommodation and volunteer services, used a number of different strategies to support the establishment and development of friendships in the lives of disabled people. Community-based recreation activities, organised by recreation workers, provided the backdrop for programs which emphasised building friendships between people with disabilities and 'normal' volunteers. The rationale for the Spastic Society's endeavours was underpinned by 'Social Role Valorisation' (and before that the principles of 'normalisation') developed by Wolfensberger (1972, 1983).

In April 1993, staff of the Spastic Society of Victoria's recreation service ('Leisure Action') and housing resource service conducted a two-day seminar to explore the experience of friendship by people with disabilities. Staff had become concerned about the loneliness and isolation experienced by people identified as having disabilities and the difficulties encountered by staff in responding to this issue. As is often the case, this forum was dominated by staff concerns regarding their professional practice and the specific techniques used in establishing and maintaining friendships in disabled people's lives.

The disabled people invited to the seminar came from a variety of backgrounds. Some were using disability services like accommodation, recreation, day centres and employment services from disability organisations such as the Spastic Society of Victoria, while others had ceased using services from the disability sector. This group of people with disabilities had experienced organisations and workers who were either unresponsive or downright destructive when it came to action in the area of friendships in their lives.

The first seminar (in April 1993), while generating a number of ideas and strategies for debate by workers, had limited benefit for the people with disabilities who attended. It did, however, provide an important impetus for a small group of people (five disabled and two non-disabled) attending the seminar to meet again at Ross House in November 1993. This smaller meeting focused solely on those people with disabilities and provided an opportunity to talk about how they maintained and developed friendships. From this meeting, the participants began to understand some of the common experiences in their lives like the lack of priority given to questions of friendship, issues of loneliness and isolation by community and disability service providers and policy-makers. They also recognised the pressing need for research to gather ideas and information about friendship and disability. Even more importantly, they 'discovered' a shared commitment to continue to meet, share experiences and work together as a group to change the way services were structured and provided. And they made this commitment in the hope that, through working together, friendships would develop that had a positive bearing on people's ongoing experience of isolation and loneliness.

Subsequent meetings of the group were held in public places with the intention of combining discussion and debate about friendship and disability with an opportunity to relax, socialise and get to know one another. There were always issues of cost and accessibility in travelling to these places, as well as the quality of the space, given the difficulties many of the members had in talking clearly. In April 1994, the group met at a tavern which was easily accessed and provided a good opportunity to relax and socialise; however, communication was significantly hampered. Even though there were very few people in the pub at the time, the table and seating arrangements, and the background noise associated with work being done to prepare for the performance of a band later that day, made it difficult for people to communicate with one another.

Given the amount of time that had passed since the group's previous meeting, the afternoon was spent going over the ideas discussed in November 1993. This provided an opportunity for new members of the group to contribute. It had the added benefit of clarifying and confirming people's motivation to be involved in what became known as the 'friendship project'. This was my [Lenny's] first meeting and the first time I had met a number of people in the group. I presented some ideas about how the research might proceed, all the time feeling somewhat overwhelmed by what might be in front of me. My journal captures my feelings:

> As I drove across town from my home in Ascot Vale to the Angel Tavern in Malvern on a Sunday afternoon in April 1994, I was acutely aware of the mixed feelings generated in me by the pending meeting. While excited by the prospect of joining the group to explore and research people's experience of friendship, I also had a number of overriding anxieties about 'getting involved' with disabled people.
>
> The first of these apprehensions concerned communication. It was five years since I had worked directly with people who I then referred to as having a 'communication impairment'. I remembered (and sometimes would prefer to forget) how debilitating it could be when I could not understand what the other person was 'saying'. I recalled the intense frustration and difficulty of maintaining that fundamental sense of commitment and respect between people when communication proved impossible. I wondered if and when the issue would arise in this group and how I would respond.
>
> The other question dominating my thinking concerned the personal commitment required in a project such as this. I wondered about where the research would lead and the expectations of group members in respect to friendship.

This meeting reinforced some of my reservations. For example, I found it extremely difficult to understand some of the people's conversation, which was partly due to the environment, but also to my inability to understand people.

During the meeting, I talked about my research interests and I asked to join the group. They said they were interested in advancing some research into disability and friendship but they had two key concerns, namely avoiding professional control of the research process and products and ensuring the relevance of the research to people with disabilities. This reaction was not surprising, given people's experience of completing countless questionnaires, surveys, individual program plans and program evaluations with little or no outcome to speak of. After some further discussion, the group recognised the benefits and welcomed my involvement.

In May 1994, the group met at the Carringbush Library in Richmond [Melbourne]. This was accessible and above all provided a quiet venue. Maree joined the group for the first time while Ingrid asked the group to consider including her partner, Robert. People indicated their support and most of the meeting time was spent listening to Ingrid and Robert describe their experience of meeting through an introduction service in a magazine. Their very personal and rich account of meeting and establishing a friendship highlighted their individual and collective strengths and their struggles. Their story also challenged the many stereotypes about disability and sexuality, and about introduction agencies, and encouraged a positive atmosphere of reflection in the group.

The group had recognised the importance of having a safe and accessible place to meet which was conducive to effective communication and provided a space to relax and socialise. The group agreed to meet at Claire's house later in May. We met one Saturday afternoon, beginning with some semi-formal discussion and finishing with an evening meal to which everyone contributed. The discussion picked up the threads of some earlier group conversations and focused on three things: the makeup of the group; how the group might go about the research; and the progress of planning a weekend away together. After listening to a number of different ideas about group composition, people concluded that ongoing changes would be disruptive, while a stable membership would assist in building trust and openness between members and a sense of group identity. We also considered the optimum size of the group and, given earlier comments and the practical issues associated with communication and translation, space and transport, identified that any more than twelve would begin to limit people's opportunity to contribute to and have a sense of being part of the group.

Questions about researching the area of friendship and disability were also discussed at this meeting. We were coming to see the value of grounding the research in people's experiences of friendship and disability, as well as the need to make time to get to know one another. It was also becoming clear that we would have to allow the research issues and ideas to emerge rather than prescribe what the issues were and how the research should progress. Finally, it was also clear that we would have to make the effort to document the research findings in a way that was accessible to people with disabilities.

Stories begin to be told

Up to the first weekend away in August 1994, the group continued to meet in one another's homes. On each occasion we set a semi-structured period for story-telling and discussion, followed by a social time for sharing a meal to which we all contributed. In many respects this decision to meet in people's homes and to have informal time to talk and share a meal together had a profound impact on people's connection and commitment to one another and to the research process. In 'sharing their homes', people disclosed a very personal part of themselves while others gained an insight into where and how another person in the group lived. Having the meetings in people's homes also provided security and safety.

The next meeting was at Arthur's flat one wintry Saturday in June. Given people's concerns about the lack of time for informal discussion, we met through the afternoon and once again finished with an evening meal. Despite our intentions to separate some of the time for socialising, the day and evening centred on people sharing and comparing life stories and experiences. Discussion initially revolved around concerns regarding a 'stuff up', with information not being sent to some group members, the organisation of the next meeting in terms of time, date and location and the availability and provision of attendant care during the weekend away in August.

Some time was then spent talking about the front-page article that had appeared that day in the *Age*. It was titled 'Parents, police fear disabled are put at risk'. In reporting the views of the parents of a disabled adult, Caroline Milburn (25 June 1994, p. 17) wrote:

In 1992 he moved out of home because his parents were too old to properly care for him. But Mr and Mrs Simm said they grew increasingly concerned that he was not getting any structured education or employment programs to occupy his days. Mr Simm said: 'He just walked the streets aimlessly, up to 35 kilometres a day. I asked him once why he went on these long walks and he said, "Because one day I'll find a friend".'

An engaging and often intense group conversation ensued, which was linked to many of the ideas presented in the newspaper article. People literally traded stories, telling of their own experiences of day centres and accommodation services in the Spastic Society of Victoria. In many respects this meeting at Arthur's began to link the individual experiences of group members and develop a group identity.

People spoke of how the organisational culture of many day centres and accommodation settings supported the lack of response by staff to the ideas and motivations of people with disabilities and reinforced apathy among staff and service users. Some stories stressed the inflexibility of those resources directed to support people's involvement in the community—like the fact that people with disabilities can only reside in accommodation funded under Commonwealth or State Disability Services legislation if they are involved in full-time employment or education, or attending a day centre or other recognised day placement on a full-time basis. All the disabled members of the group related experiences of how friendships were undermined and some told stories of the destructive reaction by staff to intimate behaviour between friends. Everyone described the confusion and frustration associated with being identified in terms of a disabled body, which was constantly compared with 'normal bodies' and ridiculed.

One month later, the group gathered on a Monday evening around 6.00 pm at Sue's temporary 'home' at the Royal Talbot hospital in Kew. She had been receiving medical treatment and living in one of the 'independent living' flats on the hospital grounds. Cassandra joined the group at this meeting. Other commitments had prevented her from attending prior meetings of the group. The group shared a meal and discussed details like the organisation and provision of attendant care, the transport to and from the venue and physical access in and around the centre, as well as the adequacy of bathroom, shower and toilet facilities.

The collective story begins to emerge

The August weekend was held in a convention centre owned by the Catholic Church and situated on the Yarra River in Lower Plenty. The group met around 8.00 p.m. on Friday evening and spent the night socialising and watching videos.

After breakfast on Saturday morning I guided the group through a meditation session which encouraged people to reflect on the nature and experience of friendships in their lives. The relaxation exercise provided an important stimulus for sharing stories and group discussion. The stories told were very powerful and deeply personal and generated a further sense of connection in the group. People relived a range of challenging, sometimes joyful but often destructive life experiences.

One important dilemma which was identified over the weekend away related to the dynamics of group discussion and, as a consequence, to the research process. The issue concerned the amount of time the group spent discussing and 'building' a collective story compared with ensuring adequate time and space for individuals to fully present particular aspects of their own lives. The dilemma was that people's personal reflections were frequently curtailed by the enthusiasm of other group members' contributions. The dynamics commonly began with one member of the group recalling a particular event in their lives which typically triggered a collage of tales and tragedies from other people which directly related to the initial topic or event. In this way, many of the details and the broader context of people's experience were either missed or glossed over.

Over the course of the weekend, the group endeavoured to address this issue by being more sensitive to 'hearing people out' when they were talking. The group became more conscious of the need to ask for more detail, provide more time and clarify whether the person communicating had completed their comments. David took on the additional responsibility of reinforcing these strategies throughout the weekend. Despite these actions and the positive influence they had on group interaction, people remained sceptical about the adequacy of the opportunities provided in the larger group for individuals to fully discuss their experiences of friendship and disability. Towards the latter part of the weekend, people divided into groups of three to five and over the course of two, three or four meetings conducted over the following seven-week period, key aspects of people's lives were researched and documented.

The group agreed that a set of questions be designed to stimulate people's reflection in these sub-groups. Claire, David, Helen and Lenny (all 'abled' group members) volunteered and ten days later met at Claire's home to develop some draft questions. These were then sent to all members of the group to consider and change as they desired. This decision to meet and talk in smaller groups in people's homes as part of the research had two important spinoffs. In the first instance, it provided a more personal environment for people to share their experiences and explore a number of significant issues not previously raised in the larger group. It also kindled more frequent contact between group members and the beginning of friendships between people.

The August weekend meeting will be remembered for a long time. Sue, Maree, Ingrid and Jenny told some horrific tales of experiences in the Spastic Society and Yooralla Special School and during visits to hospital. The dominance of doctors and therapists, the use of medication to control what staff regarded as inappropriate behaviour, the values underlying the Miss Victoria Quest and the appalling work conditions in sheltered workshops were all discussed in significant detail. Robert, Claire and I were bewildered and confused by many of their experiences that, in my reading, could almost be defined as torture. In recalling these events, Sue, Maree, Ingrid and Jenny did not dwell on their pain or the destructive impact on their lives. There was an overt sense of exhilaration in having lived through these events. As the stories were told, they seemed to gain confidence and strength in exposing the perpetrators and making connections through their experiences.

The second weekend was conducted in October and once again we met late on Friday evening. Arthur was not able to make it and Ingrid became ill a few days before the weekend, although she and Robert arrived on the Sunday and joined our discussion. A significant portion of the weekend was spent reflecting on personal experiences and consolidating the ideas and views of the group in respect to disability and friendship. Following the second weekend, a meeting was organised at Jenny's flat. The date did not suit Arthur and Melinda, while Maree was running late due to delays in getting a taxi across town.

Lots of small-group conversation happened over the dinner period. The group managed dinner successfully, with support being provided—although there was very little, if any, reference to it. It was interesting how this aspect of the group dynamics surrounding personal care had become more relaxed. After dinner, the conversation turned to talking about experiences of hospitals. This was triggered through Sue mentioning a recent conversation with her mother during her recent period of hospitalisation. Sue told how, whenever she saw the tower of St Nicholas hospital, she used to start screaming. Jenny recalled similar experiences, which in her case were triggered by seeing the overhead tramlines. She automatically associated overhead tramlines with going to the Royal Children's Hospital in Parkville. She described the process as torture and can vividly remember crying and crying as a result of the physiotherapy. Jenny recalls that she used to say to the physios as she was crying, 'You're hurting', to which the physios responded, 'It's supposed to hurt'.

Jenny commented that, in hearing the stories of other people in the group, she realised how unsupportive her own parents were. She described how her mother had constantly apologised for her. Jenny explained how she used to try to participate as much as she could with the other kids in the neighbourhood, but that when this happened her mother used to say to her, 'Don't keep them, they're only being nice to you, they don't really want to play'. Her mother's comments continually underlined the association between being disabled and being a nuisance. Jenny said that, as a result of this, her first instinct had always been to sit out of the way of others so that she wasn't a 'nuisance'. Jenny remarked that, even today, she finds it difficult to engage with others, particularly in public spaces. After hearing this, Maree scoffed at Jenny's remark. Maree had been quite amazed by Jenny's confidence—in fact, Jenny had contributed to lifting Maree's confidence.

Jenny said that, for her, 'independence was about finding your way around things'. She talked about always being on the lookout for alternative ways of getting things done. She explained how this often meant getting other people to do things for her—not in a negative sense, but in a way that people didn't mind.

Sue then raised the question of sexual abuse by asking, 'Has anyone ever thought about sexual abuse and what ideas do people have about how to respond to it?' There was a marked silence in the group for a considerable period. No one spoke. This was a significant silence given the constant banter that typified the group. I finally said, 'Well there's your answer, Sue. This is typically how people do respond—they don't talk about it and if people raise it there is silence.' Once again there was silence. David then talked about some people with disabilities accepting abuse, as the relationship with the person abusing them was often their only significant relationship. Jenny commented that she hadn't thought about these issues until she moved out and it was only then that she had to think about it. Maree commented that you didn't think about it until you were out living in the community. Little else was said; however, there was a sense that Sue's question and the topic overall remained unresolved.

The most recent meeting took place in mid-February. The agenda was to centre on the focus and future of the group. We met at my place just after lunch and once again Ingrid and Robert were unable to attend due to poor health. Arthur had another meeting and could not attend. We spent the first few hours just catching up and each person talked about what they had been doing over the New Year and January period. There were lots of interesting stories and people were very interested in what had occurred since we last met.

Some time later we got around to talking about the future and a number of directions emerged. The clearest message was that people were keen to have their stories documented. There was a powerful awareness of the significance of this process, particularly in terms of people clarifying who they were and the events, people and places that were vital in their lives. The group talked about seeking some funds to publish the stories. A second direction, which was a little more hazy, related to how people utilised their collective energies and ideas to change the way disability 'services' were constructed and delivered. Ideas were tossed around, but no concrete ideas were agreed on. Finally, people wanted to continue to meet to maintain the individual and group support that had grown and become an important part of their lives.

This story goes on. The group continues to meet, a number of autobiographies have been written and the group members are now discussing how the stories might be published in 1996–97.

Comments

This has been a story about the value of stories as a small group of people with 'disabilities' (re)capture their identity through an exemplary process of social group work.

Implicit in the stories told by these people with disabilities is the idea that groups can provide us with a sense of who we are. They can also become powerful tools for beginning to deconstruct oppressive and exploitative power relations. In telling stories in groups, we affirm our capacity to act and to assert our identity as persons and as collective actors.

In the 1990s, people are 'rediscovering' how the stories we tell about ourselves and others are fundamental to building knowledge, understanding culture, engaging in social action and affirming our identity.

Some key issues and themes

Stories

This chapter has focused on a story about storytelling. Lenny's story began with the experiences of a group of people with disabilities to illustrate the kind of group work we would like to see done. Throughout the book we look at stories, especially in the way they appear in mainstream group work as 'structured experiences', which people use to reflect on and learn from—as Lenny's group did.

Stories are important for many reasons. They matter because they are one of the ways in which we make sense of what happens to us and of who we are. Stories are usually told as narratives: they have a beginning, a middle and usually an end, in that order. Some of them are funny, some are sad and most have a point to make. They make up what we call 'history'. A lot of what is called 'social theory', or political philosophy, or science, also relies on stories. These can be narratives about history as a story of how things keep getting better and better (history as progress) or about how history is about things getting worse, or stories of how societies are full of class struggle or feminist stories about women's inequality.

Some writers go so far as to suggest that even our concept of self and our sense of being a person is nothing more than a special kind of long story which each of us writes. The stories we tell about ourselves are important for constructing, understanding, affirming and changing our identities.

Many people with serious disabilities have experienced more fully than others what it means to be dominated and marginalised. These marginalising and dominating experiences can be understood as the construction of an *identity* as dependent people. This in turn has meant the denial of *agency*.

Identity

The stories we tell have a lot to do with establishing our identity—

usually captured in names like 'wife', 'doctor', 'white', 'woman', 'male', 'homosexual', 'poor', 'Jewish' or 'prostitute', which carry a sense of social existence. Some of the names we use refer to our physical appearance—like 'big', or 'fat', or 'thin', or 'black', or 'redhead'. Sometimes they refer to bits of our history: 'I am divorced', or 'I was a boat person', or 'I was raped at sixteen'. Some of these names or markers refer to being part of a group: 'I am Catholic', or 'I am an Iraqi', or 'I am gay'.

> Identity has an inner and an outer quality. It has to do with the way we relate to and understand ourselves and with the way other people understand us and relate to us. The inner sense of identity and the outer sense of our identity are not always the same.

Our identity is made up of all of these kinds of markers that we and others use to say who we are in particular places and at particular times. Together, all of these markers can be said to help make up 'who we are' (Morris 1992).

Sometimes people say they are something or someone called an 'individual'—a concept we don't accept. It implies—and has long been used to imply—that we are all Robinson Crusoes living all alone and all by ourselves. This seems to miss some important elements of our identity—in particular, the social nature of our identity. This is so because all of those markers we just referred to imply the existence of, and the need for, other markers to make sense of the markers we have used; these other markers are also part of relationships we enter into. For instance, to be a 'doctor' or a 'teacher' we need other people—'patients' or 'students'. To be a 'man', we need other people called 'women' and 'children'. To be a 'wife', we need a 'husband' and to be a 'daughter', we need a 'parent'. To be 'fat', we need 'thin' people. To be 'human', we need 'animals' and 'vegetables'. And so on. All of the markers and names we use to name ourselves and others imply the existence of a social world of other people who are either the same or different.

All of the ways we use to describe 'self' and the ways in which we name our identity rely on the existence of others who are not the same as us. What we are *not* helps to define who we *are*. Other people with whom we have entered into a relationship also help to define who we are. And this leads to one very basic insight: our identity markers are all relational and not 'individual'. As people, we are defined by the relations we have with others (Yeatman 1992).

Sometimes, as with 'wife' and 'husband', or with 'father' and 'son' or 'daughter', these relationships are real and very close. Sometimes the relationship, like that between 'fat' and 'thin', is more conceptual and logical because 'fat' is the opposite of 'thin'. Sometimes, as in the relationship between 'working-class' and 'middle-class', the link is more abstract and structural; in other situations, such as the relationship between a 'worker' and her 'boss', it may be quite real.

The point remains that all of the identity markers do not point to or make up a 'Robinson Crusoe' individual; rather, they point to a thick texture of social relationships and to the very wide range of specific relationships that we continuously enter into throughout our lives. For this reason, we refer throughout this book to 'people' and 'persons', but not to 'individuals'.

This diverse range of relationships—and the parts of identity that they confer on us—can create a lot of tension and frustration. Identity is rarely a settled matter—to be a person who is a 'worker', a 'wife', a 'mother', 'lesbian' and a 'Catholic', for example, is to enter into a variety of relationships and a range of expectations that can be very difficult, tension-ridden and even contradictory. Thus our 'identity' may be unsettling and is often experienced as difficult. Furthermore, other people may want to define our identity in ways that are unpleasant, discriminatory or oppressive. This can be very subtle—for example, when a parent says of a young person in their hearing, 'Oh, she's such a typical teenager!' Or it may have quite sinister overtones—for instance, 'All blacks are stupid, promiscuous and drunken.' Such comments may well be experienced as a problem for our *agency*.

Agency

Agency is the idea that people are able to achieve what they want to achieve. What we have said about identity suggests that agency is not an individual quality. Agency involves the relationships we are involved in—it relies on them or is obstructed by them. The child–parent relationship, for example, is currently one in which adults can do to their children what they may not do lawfully to any other person. They may beat them or scream at them and defame them. These behaviours seriously infringe children's agency. The power of 'employers' to hire and to fire 'workers' also constrains workers' agency.

> When people have agency, it means they can make sense of, as well as initiate, influence and cope with, events in line with their own values, goals and expectations.

Groups have much to do with helping people to develop a capacity for agency. So let us explore the idea of agency in a preliminary way, and examine how groups can support agency.

Over recent decades, people have talked about how groups and group work can *empower* people, or help them to be better *citizens*. We think that these ways of talking about the goals of group work can be better described as *working to achieve agency*.

We might be able to achieve agency for ourselves by ruling our family with an iron fist, or by being a brutal boss in the office, but no one else in that setting will experience agency. Agency is a social achievement that involves the people we interact with at various levels of intimacy or distance.

Groups can support agency, but they can also impede agency. When groups are working well, they can help people affirm their identity and begin to achieve the capacity for agency. Fundamental to the notion of social agency is the idea that people are embedded in social relationships and that they actively strive for purposeful self-determination. This involves attempting to make sense of relationships, as well as initiating, influencing and coping with events in line with certain values, goals and expectations (Fryer 1995, p. 39). Agency can be achieved in specific social relations, just as it can also be undermined, restricted and frustrated by those relations. We should make no assumptions about the normal tendencies of any institutions or relationships like those found in Australia's factories, schools, offices or even in our 'family' to promote agency.

There are many different circumstances that can destroy or impede our agency. Being poor and unemployed in the 1990s is frequently experienced as destructive of our agency. As Oakley put it in 1936, the specific relationships and experiences involved in being poor or unemployed restrict, baffle and discourage people with an overwhelming 'yet indeterminate feeling of being thwarted' (Oakley 1936, p. 396). Fryer suggested that being unemployed and/or poor has two effects. First, it makes planning and forward

thinking difficult because there is fundamental uncertainty and inse-
curity in these states. Second, having little or no money also results
in corrosive stress and anxiety about all the effects of lack of
adequate income—effects like debt, power disconnection and wor-
ries about food and clothing. Relative deprivation, says Fryer, is
real. It does not take place in regard to some social scientist's
construction of a scale of normal consumption, but is referenced
against very real self-selected reference groups of friends and neigh-
bours. Within families, relative poverty translates into tortuous bud-
geting strategies, painful prioritising of differing family members'
needs, conflict-prone domestic division of financial responsibility
and coping behaviours (McGhee & Fryer 1989). There is nothing
new about these insights. Being unemployed or poor has always
been associated with anxiety and worry about not having enough
money to meet normal consumption and material needs.

Sue Kenny summarised the contemporary elements of the notion
of agency, which provides a useful checklist. These can be used to
assess institutional capabilities in both the market sector and in the
public sector to assist people to assert their agency. Among her
criteria for agency are the following;

- People have access to open and democratic structures.
- People have a real choice about their lifestyle.
- People have access to reliable information.
- People can work collectively with those who matter in their lives
  to prioritise and make decisions.
- People believe in the right to control their own destinies.
- People have the right both to participate and not participate in
  community decision-making.
- People have self-esteem and are listened to and treated with
  dignity, respect and mutuality.
- People work and live in a non-authoritarian environment. (Kenny
  1995, pp. 121–22)

All these capabilities assume a set of social relationships in a wide
range of social institutions which can facilitate experiences of
agency.

Setting up the circumstances in which agency can develop
requires that the agency be oriented to a range of logics which has
little to do with competition, exclusion and stigmatisation, and which
has much more to do with social action involving cooperation,
participation and community. Small groups of people with disabilities are struggling in the 1990s to claim and reclaim their agency

from those professions and institutions who have, in the name of 'good intentions', stripped it away. This book has been written in the belief that, through the appropriate use of groups, group facilitators can help group members achieve their own agency and recover the sense of identity upon which agency depends.

Conclusion

In selecting stories told by 'disabled' people to start the book, we are making the point that *where* we do group work is important, and with *whom* we do group work matters also. Yet too many group work texts operate on the basis that we are all the same and that we all share certain universal and essential 'human' characteristics. Furthermore, most group work texts assume that group work techniques are universal, and are applicable to anyone, anywhere. We believe it may be more useful to accept that, while we may share *some* human characteristics, our differences also need to be acknowledged and valued.

'The disabled'—people who have observable major or minor physical tremors, spasticity, loss of limbs or intellectual 'problems'—have been named in many different ways that turn some of their differences into major problems and into a powerful identity marker. Those people who *have* a disability *become* that disability (Fulcher 1989). Think of how most 'able bodied' people speak of 'the blind', 'the deaf' or 'spastics'. Why is it that people who have a cold or cancer are not called 'colds people' or 'cancerous people', while people who have a disability are turned into 'the disabled'? The 'disabled' have been defined by dominant and benevolent professional and governmental concerns as inferior, weaker and more dependent people. In some cases, they have been victims of genocide—though not here in Australia. They have faced institutionalisation, ghettoes, the development of an Australian version of *apartheid,* economic deprivation, social discrimination and eugenically inspired campaigns of sterilisation and paternalism. On the other side of the fence, since the 1970s, Australians have seen campaigns by 'disabled' collectives to claim back their identities and reshape their relations with dominant groups.

In both cases—and this is our major point—the experience and expressive capacities of being human and having agency have often been realised in group settings. As part of the attempt to redefine themselves, many 'disabled' people have renewed their collective and personal identities through group processes, which we report on here through a moving account of a year-long group process authored by researcher Lenny Jenner and members of the group.

The rest of this book explores some of the ways in which effective groups can help people to reconstruct their identities and promote their agency. We stress that group work that uses stories, that gets people to tell stories, and that gets people to reflect on their stories is going to be very powerful group work. As one Australian group worker (Williams 1991, p. 1) puts it:

> In a group run on action lines, members find a strange voice, which they may begin to recognise as their own; they feel the gush of their life building up . . . Is this who I am? They tell stories about themselves in terms of their personal or work related problems.

Group work does not have a monopoly on stories and storytelling. But as the poet Seamus Heaney (1980, p. 17) points out:

> Finding a voice means that you can get your own feeling into your own words and that your words have the feel of you about them.

Review questions

1 What is agency?
2 What is identity?
3 What are the collective stories modern Australians tell about themselves in terms of 'who we are' and 'where we come from'?
4 Can you think of other groups of people whose identity has, in a sense, been constructed for them by more powerful people?
5 What are the criteria for saying when a story told by someone is true?
6 Using Kenny's list of criteria for agency, how would you rate your household and your workplace, or some other place in which you spend a lot of time, as a place which enhances your agency?

Part II

Perspectives

2
The history of working with groups

The past is a foreign country, they do things differently there.

(L.P. Hartley 1971, p. 1)

Introduction

Working with groups can take many forms. It is something which uses different 'techniques', can have a range of perspectives and operates with many political aims and values. 'Group work' is also something that different practitioners lay claim to as a technique that they alone possess. In what follows, we reflect on the historical development of some of the ways in which professionals work with groups in Australia. To understand why group work is done the way it is in the 1990s, *and* how it might be done in the future, it is important to have some historical sense of where group work has come from. This is important because group work writers like Leslie Button have been transferred across time (1970s) and space (England) into Australian settings in the 1990s with little or no sensitivity to the issues of socioeconomic, cultural or political translation.

This chapter looks primarily at the history of group work in Australia—something that has not always been easy to write about. There is currently no published history and the sources for documenting a history of group work are scattered. People developed the elements of what became 'group work' in a range of different social settings and for different reasons, so the development of working with groups is a story of fragments that only began to look moderately coherent in the 1960s. Some would say that, even today, group work remains a fragmentary set of methods with fragmentary goals.

Our story makes the following points: in the late nineteenth century, a lot of what we now call 'voluntary work' was done by church and charitable groups. Many of these organisations worked with small groups of children, young people and working-class people, offering morally uplifting education, sporting and recreation activities (Levine & Levina 1992). The people running these organisations, who were mostly middle- and upper-class men and women, believed they knew what was best for the young and the poor, and these group activities helped ensure they got what was 'needed'.

In late nineteenth century Australia, group work was not 'professional'. It was not based on 'scientific' studies of small-group behaviour or dynamics. There were no journals with titles like *Small Group Behaviour* and no professionals claiming that their use of group work techniques defined them as such. In this period, the motive of *social control* was very strong. The charity workers (philanthropists) and 'child-savers' defined who had problems and what the beneficiaries of charity—mostly young people, the working class, and low-income people—needed. As for group work as a 'science', the professionalism and the theoretical frameworks came much later, especially in the decades after the 1950s:

> Australian group work up to the 1950s was not a body of practice informed by a 'social scientific' theory. The development of group work was rooted in the use of pastoral care and schooling practices that had been well developed by 'charity workers', teachers and preachers in which adult volunteers used small groups to introduce their charges to uplifting and morally acceptable knowledge, skills and recreational pursuits. (Interview, Hamilton-Smith 1995)

Its practitioners, however, relied on a number of assumptions about 'childhood', 'social order' or 'scientific knowledge' to 'constitute' the 'problems' which they set out to resolve, and which required the use of small groups to achieve a process of educational and moral reform. A good deal of research and action research with groups, especially that associated with Kurt Lewin, sponsored the rise of a more 'scientific' approach to working with groups. Below, we offer a sketch of the ways these ideas and approaches have informed the development of 'professionalising' ways of working with groups.

At the start, however, the people who began working with groups had no idea of where it would all end up. This story begins in

England with the establishment of 'youth work' by the 'child-savers' and later with what was called the Settlement House movement.

The 'child-savers'

Modern youth work has its origins in the work of the 'child-savers' and the 'child-saving' movement (Kett 1977; Platt 1984). The word 'child-savers' was the term used by members of the movement to describe themselves. 'Child-saving' was part of a broad nineteenth century response to 'the problem' of poverty. It rested on a belief in the need of every child to have something called a 'childhood' and was part of the process of developing a set of social practices around 'childhood' (Aries 1969). 'Child-savers' emerged in the 1860s. They ran child-care institutions, set up orphanages, went on to the streets to 'rescue' children from 'exploitative', 'negligent' and 'abusive' adults, campaigned against child labour and carried out research into children's lives (Levine & Levina 1992). In a more general sense, child-savers were one of the groups responsible for creating a separate zone in the modern life cycle called 'childhood', designed to insulate children from the adult world (Aries 1969). Child-savers were especially concerned about the hours after school, making sure recreation facilities were available that provided moral guidance and education, that kept 'idle hands' busy and minds occupied with worthy and constructive thoughts. Such activities were directed towards trying to prevent 'naturally innocent' children from discovering the evils of precocious exposure to paid work, masturbation, alcohol use, sexual experimentation or idleness. It was a prelude to the discovery and manufacture of a new stage in the life cycle called 'adolescence' (Stanley-Hall 1904).

Supervised group activities for children and adolescents became and remain a feature of most modern 'youth work'. From Sunday Schools and the first Young Men's Christian Association (1847) through to the Boy Scout movement of 1907, a plethora of youth clubs and organisations spread across Britain. All relied on the use of small groups of young people typically directed by a teacher or a 'leader' offering a range of educational activities, hobbies, sporting competitions, education and reading circles. But if 'child-savers' used groups to work with young people, the Settlement House movement was directed towards adults.

The origins of group work and the Settlement House idea

From the 1880s, Settlement Houses began to be established in many of the great cities of Britain and America (Abel 1979). Those houses offered the kinds of activities we would nowadays expect to find in community centres or neighbourhood houses (Husock 1991, pp. 16–25). The middle-class men and women who set up Settlement Houses wanted to work among the poor and the working class. Their intention was to show the poor and the young how to live 'properly' by their own moral example (Stedman-Jones 1969). The Houses themselves were usually either existing large houses in working-class suburbs or purpose-designed and built. They typically had a number of large meeting rooms as well as rooms for teaching sewing, carpentry, printing and other useful craft skills. The Settlement Houses offered reading circles and discussion groups, held lectures, and offered vocational classes in activities like carpentry and printing. They also encouraged writing and elocution exercises, staged debates and provided other uplifting activities designed to improve the morality and education of the poor (Degon 1988). These forms of group work were not therapeutic—there were no psychological techniques used, and the structuring of the small groups relied primarily on models of interaction found in the Sunday Schools and the infants schools of the nineteenth century.

Some modern versions of group work—especially those which offer activities found in neighbourhood houses, and sporting and recreational activities—have their origins in these styles of working in small groups. Unlike other forms of modern group work, which use structured exercises and draw on elaborate psychological theory and research to focus on group and individual behaviours, the content of these groups was focused on 'useful and virtuous' activities like reading, playing chess, learning a trade skill, running a debate or sometimes just having a social night with singing and elocution exercises.

Working with groups in Australia

In Australia, too, the nineteenth century saw many conscious efforts to work with groups for a number of reasons. Australian group work has its origins in a range of sporting, educational, recreational and moral activities run primarily by nineteenth century 'child-savers' and charity workers. These workers used small groups in their work with children and young people, working-class people and rural families.

Australian 'child-savers': The YMCA

The populations of the major cities like Sydney and Melbourne grew dramatically after the goldrush era of the 1850s (Davidson 1981). With industrialisation and urbanisation came the discovery of slums and poverty in the cities (Ramsland 1986). Moves to regulate the poor were not slow in coming (Landells 1983, pp. 5–10; Ramsland 1986, pp. 111–91; Kennedy 1989). The current network of youth organisations and clubs has its origins in that great nineteenth century pastoral invention, the Sunday School. Sunday Schools were an early reaction by the Christian Churches to the new 'dark and satanic mills' of early industrial capitalism.

By the 1850s, a network of clubs and organisations had been established in cities like Melbourne and Sydney to deal with what adults thought 'children' needed. Australian 'child-savers' were heavily influenced by English experience (Jaggs 1986; van Krieken 1991). As the Australian National Advisory Committee for UNESCO (1972) explained:

> Many early youth organisations were branches of London groups or looked to England as their headquarters. Groups were organised with basic English patterns either imposed or accepted.

These early organisations used small groups to supervise and teach young people how to live.

Between 1840 and 1920, New South Wales, Victoria and South Australia developed a complex of organisations including the Young Men's Christian Association (YMCA) and the Young Women's Christian Association (YWCA, established in Australia in 1884), numerous Church Brigades and other Christian youth-specific organisations. Youth clubs such as the YMCA (founded in England in 1841 by George Williams and others) and YWCA were established in most of the Australian colonies beginning with Adelaide in 1850 (Massey 1950).

The YMCA began with a commitment to Bible study (Massey 1950). It also engaged in a range of child-saving activities. By the end of the nineteenth century, most of Australia's larger cities had a YMCA, complete with gymnasium, library, extensive educational programs including lecture series, as well as drama and musical programs, sporting activities and outdoor camps—all run by a group of volunteers specialising in rescue work to get children 'off the streets'. Unlike many of today's group processes, with their therapeutic interest in developing personal skills and helping skills, these early groups had a strong teaching and activity-centred approach. These activities were run along with small groups that were directed towards developing literacy and intellectual skills through reading, discussion circles and listening to speakers talk about young people's spiritual needs. The YMCA also emphasised physical and athletic skills in organised competition for boys and later for girls.

The YMCA and YWCA emphasised the role of youth organisers or what became known as 'youth leaders'. By the end of the nineteenth century, the Boys' divisions within the YMCA were stressing the training of boys for leadership (Massey 1950, pp. 59–128; Interview, Hamilton-Smith 1995). Training youth leaders began in 1919 and was consolidated by the formation of a permanent YMCA College for Youth Leadership in Sydney in 1947. Into the 1990s, the YMCA and YWCA remain committed advocates for the use of group work techniques to achieve a variety of social goals for young people (Massey 1950).

The Try Society

Australian governments were involved early in regulating the life of children. The most significant invention of the 'child-savers' was mass, compulsory and secular state schooling, a system we still have (Barcan 1980; Theobald & Selleck 1990). By the 1870s, primary secular education was compulsory for all children in most of the Australian colonies (Connell 1980; Hunter 1994). Nowadays, most young people over the age of five are confined to these institutions for periods of up to fifteen years. As adults, many of us seem to forget our own experiences of oppressive boredom, brutality and conformism in order to continue to justify their existence. Margaret Mead recalled that, 'My grandmother wanted me to have an education so she kept me out of school'.

If mass schooling took care of most of the child's day, it didn't go far enough. A mixture of charitable and state-run 'children's welfare' was also in place in most of the 'new' Australian states to deal with 'delinquent' children (Jaggs 1986). Some of these children were placed in state-run or private reformatories for delinquent children to be re-educated. Training institutions were run, usually in the country, by a variety of Church groups, while other children were placed in foster homes to receive the kind of 'loving care' it was claimed only families could supply (see Facey 1985 for an account of what foster care could mean). In the 1880s, another burst of reforming zeal gave rise to new methods of defining 'child-saving'.

Born in 1846, William Forster was an ideal Australian 'child-saver'. He was a self-made businessman who made a fortune through trade, lived in the affluent suburb of Toorak and had eleven children. Forster's child-saving work began in a context of press reports about a wave of concern about larrikinism (McLachlan 1951). Forster's Try Society was based on the premise that city children needed saving from their sinful and immoral environment. Forster established the Try Society in 1883 after discovering three 'young larrikins' near his home. He invited them into his home to play games with his own children, and got the idea of starting a youth club. He did this in a nearby church hall (Landells 1983, pp. 5–10). By 1885, Forster had established branches of his Try Society in Fitzroy and South Yarra in well-designed, purpose-built halls. In 1886, Forster started the Little Collins Street Try Society, later better known as the Melbourne Newsboys Club. The aim of the Try Society was to offer constructive entertainment for boys who might otherwise find themselves in trouble (Landells 1983, pp. 11–30).

Like most child-saving interventions, the small groups that Forster and his volunteers ran were task-oriented. Forster believed that educational, sporting and recreational activities offered the best way of keeping boys 'off the streets' (Onians 1914). The purpose of the project was to improve the moral and social virtues of young people, and the small groups were the means to this end. The Try Society supplied a daily program of Christian chapel service, social nights with singing and elocution, gymnasium activities, classes for basic literacy and numeracy and classes in a variety of trades (especially printing, carpentry and plumbing). Picnics beside the bayside beaches were another early form of supervised social activity. The Try Society also had a large library. There were regular competitions for spelling, essay writing, marbles, musical lessons on a variety of instruments, elocution and other 'improving' activities. By 1886, Forster had also established the Try Senior Cadet Corps, which included a small brass band. The Try Senior Cadet Corps called on the services of local military personnel to train its small squad of boys. By 1890, the corps was absorbed into the local militia corps (Landells 1983, pp. 41–54).

The Boy Scouts

By the beginning of the twentieth century, these youth clubs were being augmented by a deluge of new youth groups and movements like the Pathfinders, the Boy's Militia, and the Girl Guide and Boy Scout movements.

In 1910, increasing numbers of Australian boys had had contact with Robert Baden-Powell's Scouts. That movement provided yet another model of 'child-saving', with a distinct emphasis on using small groups to educate and discipline young people. The Boy Scout statement of its policy argued in terms with which few of the diverse youth work agencies in the first half of this century would disagree:

> The characteristic method of training the scout is by admitting him a member of a desired fraternity which, guided by adult leadership, is increasingly self-governing in its successive age groups; by opening to him a succession of congenial activities and achievements in a largely outdoor setting and opportunities for service to others . . . so that he acquires competence, self-reliance, character, dependability and powers both of co-operation . . . and of leadership. (*The Policy, Organisation and Rules of the Boy Scout Assoc,* London 1959 par. 1(ii))

Scouting incorporated a set of techniques and processes intended to shape the moral character of the young person. The Scouting movement stressed moral qualities like obedience, self-reliance, loyalty, public service, dependability and cooperativeness, summarised in terms of taking an oath to uphold the Scout Law. Many participants in these early 'youth groups' became and remained devoted practitioners of various early styles of group work, much of which developed around sporting and recreational activities.

If nineteenth century 'youth clubs' used small groups as a primary basis for securing young people's social and moral virtue, then other educative interventions like the adult education movement also played a part in the history of group work in Australia.

The adult education movement

Adult education was another important sponsor of the early use of groups for the purposes of educational and moral uplift. Adult education had a number of sponsors and institutional locations in the second half of the nineteenth century (Badger 1979). Most of the colonies supported a network of Mechanics' Institutes, which provided a basic library service in the suburbs and country towns (Nadel 1957). From the 1850s, the nascent union movement began to push for expanded adult education opportunities for union members and Working Men's Colleges provided a strong foundation for vocational and technical education (Murray-Smith & Dare 1987). The universities provided yet another dimension, with their commitment to extension activities.

The university extension system 'for adult learners, also used groups as aids to educational and technical enrichment' (Williams 1972). In England in the 1840s, the practice of 'adult education' developed through a system of university-run 'extension activities'. This meant that adults attended universities in the evening to study for a non-degree course on a part-time basis. The 'extension' system used innovations like the provision of a printed syllabus, the preparation of essays by the student and the use of small discussion groups after a lecture (what we now call 'tutorials'). The novelty of this lies in the fact that 'proper' universities in England and Australia until the 1960s used only a combination of mass lectures and examinations (or, if you were at Oxbridge, a one-to-one tutorial with a college tutor).

Sydney University, at the behest of Walter Scott, introduced the first extension lectures in 1886; by 1895 they were a feature of each Australian university. As Williams notes, they were not a reaction to widespread community pressure for these activities (Williams 1972, p. 190). At the University of Melbourne, sponsors like Alfred Deakin and H.B. Higgins promoted a program which attracted 2018 students by 1892, or three times the formal undergraduate population. The program offered studies in classical, human and social sciences, while abstaining from any interest in vocational curricula. The movement also supported a growth in public library activities, as well as providing a new market for British publishers (Williams 1972, pp. 200–204).

But by the start of the twentieth century it was in trouble. It was criticised on the grounds that most of its extra-mural students were middle- and upper-class people, and that its courses were not 'practical' enough—criticisms which came to be increasingly accepted as valid (interview, Hamilton-Smith 1995).

In 1903 in England, and in response to similar criticism, Mansbridge started the Workers' Education Association (WEA), designed to attract working-class people to adult education. The WEA offered small groups or 'tutorials' as the basic teaching device and three-year programs. By 1910 it was a raging success and William Temple, its national president (and also later Archbishop of Canterbury and the man who created the phrase 'the welfare state' in 1942), visited Australia to spread the word. Soon afterwards, the WEA was established in every state except Western Australia. A partnership between universities and the WEA drew on trade union membership. The WEA provided classes that were taught by university staff and that used curricula designed by the WEA and universities (Williams 1972, p. 209). The WEA became a strong force for a democratic model of adult education after 1918. The extension system and the WEA provided experiences in the use of small groups. As Mansbridge urged, without education:

> . . . some individuals will drift hither, thither, cooperating not with the forces which build, but with those that destroy. If Education be not allowed its opportunity, ignorance will have its revenge. (Cited in Williams 1972, p. 206)

Rural education

Running in parallel with these urban networks was the Agricultural Bureau movement, a South Australian and New South Wales government-sponsored system of adult education for farmers and their families. Its goals also included advocating improvements in the practices of farmers (see article in *The Australian Encyclopaedia,* 1958). This movement was equivalent to many other movements, like the Mechanics Institute movement, that were aimed at improving the intellectual and moral calibre of citizens within Australia's colonial cities.

South Australia was the first colony to establish a Bureau of Agriculture in 1888. The government accepted advice from Albert Molineaux to establish a system of educational extension activities run from a central office with a paid secretary and a board of experts (Hirst 1973, pp. 52–57). Its mission was to support the spread of scientific information on a range of farming and grazing practices and so assist farmers and graziers to increase their productivity and adopt proper—that is, 'expert'—farming practices. The central bureau was also to be responsible for creating a network of local bureaux. Within 25 years, South Australia had a network of 155 branches and 3500 members. By 1954 there were over 324 branches with a membership of 11 747. Women's branches were formed first in 1917; by 1954, there were 80 women's branches (Hirst 1973).

New South Wales followed suit in 1910 and the first state conference was held in 1923 at Hawkesbury College. At its peak, New South Wales had over 900 local bureau branches, each heavily subsidised by the Central Bureau in Sydney so as to enable it to carry out local research and education extension activities.

The Agricultural Bureau was a rural version of adult education. Its workers believed that by mobilising small groups of farmers and their families, and encouraging them to form small local groups, farmers and their families would be receptive to, and keen to apply, expert knowledge and expert solutions to expert-defined problems. By the late 1940s, the University of New England at Armidale (in northern New South Wales) became a major centre for sponsoring and training workers in the Agricultural Bureau movement. It also became a major centre for the development of small-group education and training (interview, Hamilton-Smith 1995).

The strands of modern group work in Australia

Australian group work had its origins in a range of sporting, educational, recreational and moral activities run primarily by nineteenth century 'child-savers' and charity workers. These workers used small groups in their work with children and young people, working-class people and rural families. While there are still continuing versions of these kinds of group work, the distinctive features of modern group work include such things as its increasing reliance on scientific research and theory, and its use by professional human service workers. If enthusiastic amateurs in the late nineteenth century developed early forms of working with groups, in the 1990s this has become an increasingly professionalised activity. Today, group work has become a part of modern professionalism. It helps if one places the evolution of group work styles and techniques in the context of the enormous recent growth in the human service professions—a growth which is itself part of what many people today call the emergence of a 'post-industrial society'.

The growth in the second half of the twentieth century in the numbers of groups calling themselves 'professional', and in the numbers of people working as human service 'professionals', has led writers like Perkins (1991) to call this the 'century of the professions'. Other writers, who see the 'helping professions' as very unhelpful—like Ivan Illich—have called our epoch the 'age of disabling professions' (Illich 1983). The history of group work lies in the changing relations between professional and occupational activities, the broader framework of modern societies and in the 'discovery' of particular social problems (like unemployment, poverty, delinquency, sexual abuse and 'mental illness').

Professionalism

'Professionalism' is one of the most widely used words in the twentieth century. The term 'professional' is used to claim a certain authority and power based on the 'fact' that someone is an expert. To be a 'professional' is to claim that you have both an intellectual background and a high level of practical expertise and specialist knowledge. People who claim to be professional tend to use it more than anyone else and they are the also people who offer 'descriptions' of what it means to be a professional.

Basic to the self-description of many professions is the idea that professionals are motivated by *altruism* (that is, they are self-sacrificing), rather than by self-interest. (On 'charity', see Stedman-Jones 1969.) Sociologists like Parsons and Merton (who are themselves professionals) argue that the ever-expanding army of professionals has helped make modern society a more caring, more moral, more rational and more scientific place than would otherwise have been the case.

The alleged characteristics of a professional

Professionals are said to have the following characteristics:

- Professional work is grounded in a body of theoretical and scientific knowledge received through a higher education institution.
- Professionals are certified to possess practical expertise and experience before they start to practise.
- Professionals belong to a professional body (like a society or association) that safeguards entry to the profession and sets the standards of knowledge and practice.
- Professionals put service to others (*altruism*) ahead of their own self-interest.
- Professionals have a Code of Ethics to inform their practice.
- Professionals exercise relative autonomy.

The esteem enjoyed by professionals, however, has impacted on those who do group work, especially given the fact that many of those who practise group work also see themselves as professionals.

Most of those who 'do' group work, or who use group work today, claim professional status and expertise. Group work has become a standard tool of trade for a variety of human service work carried out by professionals, semi- or unskilled workers and by an army of voluntary workers. But group work has also acquired a radical reputation (Epstein 1970, pp. 123–31; Rothman 1974, pp. 97–98). That this has been possible speaks to the power of science.

Science and small groups

The first four decades of the twentieth century saw what was initially small-scale social scientific interest in the nature and dynamics of small groups in America, England and Europe develop into a significant research theme. Most of the international social scientific research on small groups has been characterised by a belief in the desirability and possibility of 'measuring' social interactions in groups. This idea relies on the 'positivist' assumption that human behaviour is predictable, and therefore amenable to such treatment in the same ways that physical entities are in the natural world.

New Education Fellowship

In Australia, this interest in a scientific approach to working with people had at least one expression, in the growth of what became known as the New Education Fellowship. The New Education Fellowship was an international movement initiated in 1921 to promote new educational ideas and reforms (Selleck 1968). It was a movement directed towards educational reform, finding an enthusiastic reception among the burgeoning Australian university-based teacher training colleges. The leading international figures of the New Education Fellowship included people like Montessori, Ensor and Dewey and, in Australia, K.S. Cunningham and Professor G.S. Browne. Their stated aim was to promote a progressive and liberal democratic reconstruction of society through the medium of a new education (Rowse 1978). This advocacy joined with the promotion of the new social sciences, especially psychology and psychoanalysis, which helped renovate teaching as a professional activity—grounded in university training and 'proper scientific study'.[1]

While Australian universities established a role for psychology research and teaching in the late nineteenth century, Australian academic psychology demonstrated little interest in sponsoring research into group dynamics. The main growth in formal academic and professional psychology took place during and after the 1940s, and again group research did not figure at all. Most of the research and teaching in this period emphasised a number of different themes which did not include the work being done on small groups in England, America and Europe. Building on psychology degrees initially offered at Sydney University (in the 1920s) under Lovell, and at the University of Western Australia (in the 1930s), psychology degrees were established at Melbourne University in the 1940s under O.E. Oeser. Most early development of psychology was connected to the growth in teacher training.

The New Education Fellowship strongly emphasised community education, a prelude to the later projects of establishing 'community centres' through the war years (1939–45) and in the postwar reconstruction project (Rowse 1978). The New Education Fellowship and the commitment to the idea of community centres represented a burgeoning interest in Australia in coordinating social scientific research, professional training and the reform of traditional educational practices in the name of promoting citizenship and lifelong adult education (Rowse 1978). These expressions of interwar liberalism underwrote a postwar interest in the systematic use of small groups as a tool for education, youth work and therapy. An equivalent move was already underway in Europe and North America, in regard to research into the nature of small groups. This research impacted heavily on 'psychology, social psychology, psychiatry, sociology, political science, and anthropology, applied mathematics, cybernetics, and general system theory' (Mills 1970).

The focal point for much of the New Education Fellowship's advocacy was the idea of a new compact between 'individual' and 'society', a theme which was to be developed by some forms of modern group work, which identifies the need for the 'individual' to be 'integrated' into society. The themes of integration and social cohesion have been important notions underlying the development

---

1   This was a code word for the promotion of progressive eugenic research into individual differences like physical and intellectual 'fitness' which most progressive educators, medical men, psychologists and social scientists supported until 1939.

of modern theories of group work, especially—as we will show—in the hands of theorists like Lewin.

The twentieth century idea of 'socialisation' has provided a foundation for the modern practice of some forms of group work, referred to as 'remedial perspective' in Chapter 3. According to this account, the 'individual' internalises the appropriate behaviours and values of his or her society through effective socialisation. However, the occurrence in some people of behaviours identified as maladjusted or deviant is also seen as a normal phenomenon. Group work has been used as a tool for assisting with this socialisation process.

Researching the small group

Significant early theoretical work that focused on the nature of small groups was done by German theorist Georg Simmel in the years 1902–17. (His work was not directly influential and was 'rediscovered' several times throughout the twentieth century.) In 1909, the American Charles Cooley drew attention to the key role played by what he called 'primary groups', like the family or the kindergarten, in helping to 'socialise' human beings.

Australian-born anthropologist Elton Mayo developed a number of fundamental insights in the 1930s, when he demonstrated that industrial output was affected by the quality of relationships among American workers. Mayo and his colleagues, Roethlisberger and Dickinson (1939), made this observation in a project organised through the Harvard Graduate School in Business Studies in the 1920s and 1930s, and they carried out pioneering studies at the Hawthorne plant of the Western Electric Company (Mayo 1933). The Mayo team asked how groups of workers experienced their employment and discovered that when workers felt management were interested in them as human beings, they responded positively.

Roethlisberger and Dickinson (1939) published the findings of this discovery that underpinned the development of the Human Relations model from the 1940s on. Building on Mayo's work, psychologists like Carl Rogers developed T-Groups (T stands for Training) to 'sensitise' managers to the human needs of their workers.

Kurt Lewin (1890–1947)

The outstanding figure in the history of research into groups, however, was undoubtedly social psychologist Kurt Lewin (1890–1947).

Lewin provided considerable impetus for the evolution of group work research through the 1930s and 1940s and pioneered the scientific–experimental study of groups central to the development of a social science of group dynamics. Lewin worked first at Berlin University with other members of the Gestalt group (Wertheimer and Kohler) before emigrating in 1933 to America, where he took a post at Cornell and later at Massachusetts Institute of Technology (MIT), where he established the Research Centre for Group Dynamics. His early work on groups of young children in the late 1930s convinced him that different styles of leadership (ranging from autocratic to democratic styles) in groups affected the ways these groups worked.

Lewin insisted on the use of experiential learning techniques for training people in group work. For Lewin, examining and reflecting on one's own experiences provided the basis for evaluating practices and ideas. Lewin believed in learning through experience and actively practised experiential learning in the development of his own theories on group work (Lewin 1947). This theme has become a central part of most modern group work practice, working to both 'remedial' and 'reciprocal' perspectives (see Chapters 3 and 4).

Lewin also believed that it was appropriate to use the 'experimental' method of 'proper science' in his own research. Experiment, practice and empiricism were considered vital for informing good theory and practice. According to Lewin, such processes provided a way of testing theory against 'reality'. Theory was valued by Lewin and was considered necessary for an understanding of social action and intelligent practice. Conversely, Lewin argued that practice was necessary for the development of sensible theory (Lewin 1951). Many of these themes have been taken into the heartland of modern group work theory.

Lewin's model set the scene for the development of the later view found among many group workers that all groups go through certain fixed stages in a life cycle (see Chapter 5). Lewin's account of effective group work envisaged sets of corkscrew or spiral phases of development. Each stage of the process involves collective decision-making about the kinds of changes or improvements that the group is to work towards. This initial move provokes information-gathering activity, or a research process into the particular areas of concern. Having done this, the group then reflects on its progress and considers what other strategies are required. The plan is based on what the group thinks is the best way to achieve the desired change. The plan is then divided into smaller parts that can be accomplished relatively easily. Before the first section or part of the plan is undertaken, agreement is sought about how to further monitor and evaluate the process. The first stage then begins. Once this initial stage of the group's activities is underway, ideas about how to monitor and evaluate the group's progress begin to be developed. Reflection on the initial phase of the group's activities provides the basis for developing new plans, directions and procedures. With this new data on hand, the overall plan is reconsidered and amended and the next phase of action in the project developed (Lewin 1947).

Lewin's protégés, like Festinger, Schacter and Bach, tested the effects of group cohesion on pressure to conform to group norms. They and their successors confirmed that, when an experimental group is established to brutalise an individual member of a group, that individual can be persuaded to believe, say or do many outrageous things. (The fact that this was done inside an experimental setting does not lead to the conclusion that groups outside the experimental setting will 'experience' the same effect.)

There has been no tradition of small group research in Australia—a literature search carried out for the writing of this book reveals only a thin research output. If any one group can claim credit for the 'scientific' development of group work, American writers would have the strongest claim. In North America from 1890 to 1940, there was a continuous growth of academic interest in small groups, beginning with one study in 1890, and extending to over 30 studies in 1940. The major impetus for research into groups came in the 1920s and 1930s and was undoubtedly stimulated by Lewin and his colleagues. By the late 1940s, there were about 55 major studies appearing each year—a number which increased dramatically to over 150 in the late 1950s before settling back to a persistent rate of around 125 studies per year in the 1960s.

In the early 1950s, work done by the sociologist Bales (with Parsons and Shils in the background) developed a sociological theory of group interactions plus an 'empirical' scoring technique (Bales 1950). Bales' work confirmed the drift towards universalising group processes and seeing 'individuals', as being constrained to act in predictable ways in all groups. Homans' work (1950; 1961) confirmed this trend. Bales, however, tended to reduce the stress on the idea of the 'group' versus the 'individual'. Bales argued that groups were mini-social systems and therefore had to address the universal problems all such social systems allegedly confronted (like how to adapt to the realities of a situation; how to accomplish group goals; how to meet members' needs and the like). Bales claimed that the same dynamics were at work everywhere, all the time and irrespective of who was in the group. These themes were further developed by Cartwright and Zander, whose text on group dynamics (Cartwight & Zander 1960) became the dominant one of the 1960s and 1970s in Australia for the nascent professional group workers.

Group psychotherapy began to make its mark in the late 1940s and 1950s as therapists like Wolf, Semrad and Bion developed a body of theory and practice that dealt with the use of groups as aids in the treatment of psychosis. At the same time, Semrad began to use group processes as a way of teaching about group dynamics. At Harvard, Semrad organised a series of seminars where a seminar group met, observed its own group processes and group members interpreted to each other what was happening. As Mills put it:

> . . . it is becoming increasingly apparent that such groups are a revolutionary departure, in the sense that they are a new order of social system. The collective purpose of their members is to learn about their collective experience. Goals preoccupying other groups are set aside so the group is free to develop an awareness of itself, to discover what its 'self' is, where the 'self' means the group. Such groups have a built-in potential for becoming self-aware, self-knowing systems . . . (Mills 1967, p. 7)

At the National Training Laboratories in Washington, and later at Bethel, Maine, Rogers and his colleagues presented some of the elements of the T-Group, which provided executives, scientists and teachers using group processes with insights into themselves and group dynamics. This work was to find its mark in Australia through the development of both industrial psychology and the moves to professionalise youth work training in the postwar period after 1945.

Psychology, industrial psychology and group work

Interest in group processes after 1945 reflected a preoccupation with vocational guidance and was also symptomatic of the shift to professionalise human services. Mayo at the University of Queensland (as Professor of Philosophy until he left for Harvard) taught psychology. However, industrial psychology as a separate entity began in 1927, when Martin established the Australian Institute of Industrial Psychology to develop tests for vocational guidance to be used in New South Wales.

Dunnette claims there have been four phases in the evolution of industrial psychology in Australia:

From 1930 to 1941 was the heyday of tests and job analysis. The second era, 1942 to 1955, was the era of service to management. The stress was on human relations, morale and satisfaction, rating and aptitude scales, training and factor analysis. The third stage, from 1956 to 1969 was the era of the humanisation of work and more understanding of human diversity and individuality, and a new interest in motivation and in organisational impact. The fourth since then has dealt with future shock. (Dunnette 1972, pp. 31–40)

Psychology in Australian universities was only really consolidated after 1945. Most of the foundation Chairs in psychology were created in the 1950s and 1960s in the eighteen universities that then existed (O'Neill 1977, pp. 18–19). An Australian branch of the British Psychological Society was created in 1945, giving way in 1966 to the Australian Psychological Society (APS). This society established formal control over entry to the profession via standards and curriculum guidelines for the psychology degrees which all Australian universities currently offer. The development of intelligence and aptitude tests, and a number of applied interventions in the areas of education and vocational guidance, was central to Australian psychology.

In Australia from the late 1940s, a small body of psychologists working for the Australian government as industrial psychologists began incorporating the insights of small-group research and the sensitivity training techniques developed in Washington at the National Training Laboratory by Carl Rogers and others. (This work was funded by corporate Americans like General Motors.)

Later, between 1965 and 1970, the Commonwealth Department of Labour and Immigration established a training program for new and continuing staff, using its own psychologists to develop the program. This was based on Carl Rogers' T-Groups (Howe 1977, pp. 128–35). By the late 1960s, the Personnel Practice Section employed over 70 psychologists, some of whom were using group techniques for training purposes in the Commonwealth Public Service. There was also a strong emphasis on experiential learning conducted by an outside group leader, which included communication exercises, encounter sessions and role-playing exercises as members 'played' clients who had presented them with particular problems. This program was influenced by the work of Rogers (1965), Truax and Carkhuff (1967) and Carkhuff (1969).

Carkhuff, in particular, persuaded the Department that interpersonal communication skills were more important than ability to administer aptitude tests. The training program therefore emphasised experiential learning of skills built around interviewing, listening and feedback behaviours. This established a pattern soon copied by state public services, which used psychologists skilled in Rogerian group work techniques to develop and implement inservice training programs for public servants. Through the 1970s, these group workers spread their skills inside the public sector and then throughout the community and the private corporate sector. By the early 1970s, these group workers were running private training sessions for people interested in 'self-development' or in group dynamics at places like the Bouverie Street Clinic in Melbourne.

The development of therapeutically oriented group work from the early 1960s reflected the consolidation of Australian psychology and the fact that there was now a regular supply of new graduates. The establishment of new universities and Colleges of Advanced Education (CAEs) in the 1960s and the early 1970s supported a constant growth in undergraduate enrolment in psychology courses, many of which, under the guidance of the APS and new legislation controlling psychological practices, provided the basis for group work practices in the new universities and CAEs.

There does not appear to have been a comprehensive Australian base for small-group research. Most of the theoretical impetus came from American texts by Rogers and Carkhuff, which stressed an applied approach to learning, developing and applying interpersonal skills and using group techniques.

These developments affected a number of other professionals, who began developing group work in the welfare and service sector as practitioners moved from a more traditional 'casework' emphasis (dealing with individual cases) towards a focus on having people working within their own 'self-help groups'. Examples of this shift could be seen in the 1960s and 1970s with the development of Alcoholics Anonymous, the Council for the Single Mother and her Child, and the Civilian Widows' Association. In each instance, autonomous self-help groups were established and supported by practitioners to reduce isolation and to encourage identity as a member of a group with shared interests. While youth work was not the only human service profession to embrace group work, its development in a sense is symptomatic of the modern evolution of a 'professional' model of group work.

Group work, welfare and youth work

Crucial to the moves being made in the 1960s to upgrade and professionalise were efforts made in the training of youth workers. In this process, group work came to be defined as a central skill and a core component of the professional curriculum.

Until the late 1970s, the YMCA was the primary provider of youth work training and education in Australia. Central to its program was the training of 'youth leaders' skilled in small group processes. In Sydney, the YMCA established a permanent College for Youth Leadership in 1947. This offered a two-year course in collaboration with the Extension Studies Board of Sydney University. Between 1947 and 1963, 124 students were admitted and 78 graduated before the college was relocated to Melbourne in 1964. This course was now formally offered by the Youth Council of Victoria and taught by the YMCA (Hamilton-Smith & Brownell 1973).

There had been some previous attempts to establish youth work on a professional basis—which meant a university-based course of study. In 1944, the first quasi-professional youth work course in Australia was offered in Melbourne as part of an 'emergency' training program offered at the Department of Social Studies at the University of Melbourne (Szirom & Spartels 1995). The course was the product of a collection of Melbourne-based middle-class, progressive professionals, centred around the University of Melbourne. A meeting of these people urged the creation of a youth work course. This initiative included NEF educationists (Professor G.S. Browne and Fritz Duras), the Vice-Chancellor of Melbourne University (J.G. Medley), social workers (Jocelyn Hyslop) and enthusiasts for National Fitness (like Swires and Featonby). The group drew from a mixture of what was known as the Big Eight youth organisations. This included representatives of Church organisations, the YMCA and YWCA and the Victorian Association of Boys Clubs (Hamilton-Smith & Brownell 1973).

This ten month long 'emergency' program was 'incorporated into the Diploma of Social Work when it was extended to three years and a group work option developed' (Szirom & Spartels 1995, p. 7). Group work education briefly became a mainstay of the emergent social work educational programs which were established in the Universities of Sydney, Melbourne and Adelaide in the postwar period, before they disappeared in the 1950s only to be resuscitated in the 1960s (Hamilton-Smith & Brownell 1973).

Group work as a component of youth work was associated with moves to formalise the training and education of youth workers. From the 1950s, training in group work skills amongst youth workers (most of them working in the sport and recreation movements) involved techniques for working with young people in team activities and group programs. Practitioners working with young people in a variety of fields found that 'natural' groups could be respected and redirected towards positive outcomes and shared activities. These recreational group workers could offer an understanding of the differences inherent in the stages of group formation and generated skills in managing the entry into and relationships of the group members within the total group process. Church and welfare groups found that their service objectives could be structured and legitimised by adopting elements of group dynamics.

By the 1960s, the pressure to upgrade youth work and make it a professional activity (along with other occupational groups like teaching) was mounting. In the early 1960s there were only 119 designated full-time 'youth workers' in Victoria, and of these one-third were employed by the YMCA, YWCA and the Victorian Association of Youth Clubs. These workers worked alongside thousands of volunteer youth workers (interview, Hamilton-Smith 1995).

Educationists, workers and researchers like W.F. Connell and Ellery Hamilton-Smith pressed insistently for a 'professional' training program for youth workers from 1963–64. Connell, for example, argued that the youth worker was:

> . . . in essence a teacher [who] should understand both the business of educating and the development of youth who are his [sic.] special responsibility and he should be skilled and practised in his own kind of teaching. (Connell 1964, p. 3)

Between 1964 and 1966, the first modern course in youth work was designed and implemented by the Social Welfare Training Council of Victoria. This was a two-year Diploma in Youth Leadership course, which became a three-year course after 1970. Its first director, Vern Davies, encouraged the teaching of group work to the first three intakes, which attracted a number of students who already had extensive practice experience in Victoria's youth organisations. Carl Rogers' 1963 tour of Australia further aroused the interest of local youth workers and educators and trainers in group work (interview, Hamilton-Smith 1995).

It is worth noting here that group work practices and themes briefly became a popular phenomenon in the late 1960s and early 1970s, as enthusiasm for sensitivity training and encounter groups became part of a middle-class 'counter-culture'. This emerged from a combination of psychotherapist groups, social consciousness-raising groups, encounter groups and social control groups popularised by middle-class practitioners intending to release individuals from their past neurotic or repressed behaviours and 'victim' status.

This was the era of the 'counter-culture' in Australia. It was a period when the suburbs around major Australian universities were host to a peculiar blend of liberation rhetoric, psychotherapy and sexual politics. The 'counter-culture' developed initially from a rejection of the Australian government's use of conscription to 'man' its military intervention in Vietnam between 1966 and 1972. This merged into a combination of oppositional forces to what were seen as the oppressive effects of 'mainstream life'. It was a force fuelled also by new drugs, music of resistance, and alternative clothes and hairstyles. Having identified the 'repressive' effects of traditional middle-class forms of education, child-rearing members of the 'counter-culture' then rediscovered the theories of people like Wilhelm Reich. They also supported the work of therapists like Schultz, Rogers, Maslow and Janov (Rogers 1969). The common theme related to the very old romantic story that people were born naturally happy, equal and healthy. Society and civilisation were the problems—in particular, the pressures to conform that were especially strong in family life, schools, kindergartens, universities, mass advertising and modern bureaucratic organisations.

Counter-culturalists like Roszack (1974) argued that mainstream society, with its consumerism, work ethic and living in 'dull' suburban households, deformed our human potential, repressed people and made them unhappy, conservative and unhealthy. To recover the Natural Man/Woman, the 'counter-culture' recommended a variety of techniques. These included the use of mind-altering drugs (like LSD) or drugs like marijuana, various psychological therapies including group therapies of various kinds, and behavioural therapies like Reichian therapy. Stress was placed on the 'need' to 'recover' one's full orgasmic capacity. Primal screaming or rebirthing could also 'cure' people of their neuroses and help people experience political, sexual and social liberation. This was also often seen as part of developing radical politics.

Such group work practitioners placed a heavy emphasis on becoming aware of 'the collective' or common origins of personal feelings, beliefs and behaviours (Shaw 1971). Examples of this process included the use of T-Group processes at the Bouverie Street Clinic in Carlton (Victoria) in the early 1970s, where—on a volunteer basis—professional trainers ran weekend sessions for fee-paying volunteers to have an encounter experience. The first generation of the Women's Movement in Australia also developed early versions of 'consciousness raising' (CR) groups. Small numbers of men also participated in establishing and running men's consciousness-raising groups.

The first intakes in the Welfare Institute course included people like Tricia Szirom, John Harris and Roger Trowbridge, who went on to develop notable careers in group work practice (interview, Trowbridge 1995). This course made group work the core component of the curriculum and it was taught throughout the course. Students were allocated to syndicate groups which were then asked to develop group projects, attend lectures, engage in a small number of structured experiences and perform research on groups, as well as integrate this material with the field work. The curriculum was grounded in the work of Rogers and the account of group dynamics found in Cartwright and Zander (1960). Following a six-week strike during which students expressed concern about the standards and conservatism of the program, a pledge to review the course was made (interview, Trowbridge 1995). In 1970, the Welfare Institute course, now headed by a psychiatric social worker named Michael Clark, became a three-year course.

Concern continued to be expressed that neither the YMCA course nor the Welfare Institute course were located in a university, nor were they recognised as having professional status; pressure mounted again in 1974–75 for a professional course. Ellery Hamilton-Smith's enthusiasm for a professional model of youth work and its educational preparation remained strong. Hamilton-Smith's informal leadership of the field was widely acknowledged, and he was commissioned to carry out a consultation with workers and analysis of youth work in Victoria. His report (*Youth Workers and their Education*, 1975) reflected the results of that consultation. Following negotiations between the YMCA, the Social Welfare Institute and several tertiary institutes, it was decided to transfer the YMCA course to the Coburg Teachers' College, which would offer the long-desired professional course in youth work.

Both the Social Welfare course and the YMCA course were

phased out in 1980 to make way for the new Coburg Teachers' College course. (This became the Philip Institute course and is now the Royal Melbourne Institute of Technology—RMIT—course.) Initially the course was a two-year diploma program before being turned into a three-year degree in 1982. Group work was a core part of this first 'professional' tertiary youth work course in Australia, with two semesters of group work being a compulsory part of the course (interview, Hamilton-Smith 1995). A dominant view of staff teaching the RMIT program is that group work is what distinguishes youth work from other welfare programs.

While the YMCA reduced its commitment to youth work and group work, the YWCA has continued working in the area. In the 1980s, under the direction of Tricia Szirom, the YWCA developed group work programs for women which were concerned with dealing with sexism in the workplace and women's managerial and organisational skills.

In South Australia, between 1967 and the late 1970s (when it disappeared), the South Australian Institute of Technology (SAIT) established a Youth Work Certificate course inside its Social Work Department. One-third of the course was devoted to group work, covering topics like leadership, attitudes, norms, roles, group structure, group work techniques, T-Group, learning theory, transactional analysis (TA) and problem group techniques. Another youth work program is provided by Edith Cowan University in Perth. This has been offered since 1990 and also provides group work training. Group work education in other human service courses is found in a number of other professional and occupational faculties around Australia. For example, teacher training faculties have developed their own model of small-group processes. Community development and social work courses have likewise found room for their versions of group work, and counselling and psychology courses also have a range of therapeutic group processes available.

Conclusion

As the practices and knowledge bases of the various 'histories' of group work have evolved, the boundaries between these streams have blurred. Interest has shifted to such common concerns as 'leadership' and 'fellowship', 'self-directed teams' and the adoption of group work and community development practices. Knowledge about group processes has also become transferable to diverse settings. The human resource–human capital interests of business have begun to use this expertise. Executive development programs have adopted the patterns of Outward Bound programs to become Team Skills Development. Psychotherapeutic groups became 'Quality Circles'. Exploration groups became negotiating preparation sessions.

It is not possible to survey all of the forms group work now takes or all of the perspectives and techniques that now characterise it. It is, however, worth making one point again: *You cannot assume that group work involves just one technique or that it is based on one set of political or moral objectives.*

Review questions

1 What are some of the main factors that have shaped Australian group work?
2 What were some of the primary motives underlying the use of groups in Australia?
3 Do you think the qualities often used to describe a 'professional' person actually describe those groups you call 'professional' (lawyers, doctors, academics, social workers, etc.)?
4 Is professionalism (e.g. in group work) that is based on 'scientific' training always going to be a problem for the agency of the clients or the customers of those professionals?
5 What kinds of criteria would you use to check out the claims of modern group workers to be able to 'empower' people?

3
Working with groups:
Remedial and reciprocal perspectives

Introduction: What is group work?

How are we to understand working with groups? Can we make sense of groups by generalising about all 'groups'? Is there a single, over-arching model or theory of groups? Many textbooks begin with a simple definition of something called 'group work', as if it is possible—at least in principle—to come up with a single, simple definition. Take a standard 'definition' like that offered by Brown (1991, p. 4):

Group work

Group work is a generic term for all kinds of professional work with groups. It is used to describe an array of approaches from education, recreation, social work, psychology, and related helping professions. The basic ingredient in group work is that the worker enables group members to engage in collaborative problem solving.

Such a definition purports to be very general; however, it is actually quite narrow and overly restrictive. Can you identify why this supposedly general 'description' of all groups really only addresses *some* of the ways in which group work is done?

There are many answers to the question 'what is group work?' Some relate to dominant assumptions about certain groups and the ways in which professionals—teachers, youth workers, social workers, community workers and the like—work with groups. But we should begin by asking ourselves how we can, or *whether* we can, make sense of groups as a single social phenomenon. Is there a single, over-arching model or theory of groups? For example, can we use a notion like 'life-cycle' (borrowed from Erikson's account of the alleged eight Ages of Man) and apply similar models to groups by assuming comparable stages of development (Erikson 1963)?

Or can we discuss groups in the way Crawley meant when he referred to the coexistence of the 'task realm' and the 'maintenance realm' in all groups (Crawley 1978)? Or should we—as so many texts advise—start describing things like 'leadership styles', 'techniques of group work', 'modes of communication' and 'goal setting' as though a single set of categories, typologies and technical approaches can be used to develop a theory and a model of practice for group work? We have reservations about the value of many of these approaches, especially those which produce abstracted descriptions and discussions about something called 'the group' or 'doing group work'. This is what Tom Douglas sets out to do when he asserts that social group work groups are a:

> member of the family of groups. This means that what all groups have in common is probably much more fundamental to the understanding of group behaviour than the differences to which so much attention is given. (1988, p. 1)

Douglas, then, can insist that:

> the functions of all groups, defined as the way they operate, are identical and . . . it is not so much the absolute difference of function that creates apparent difference in groups, but the intensity, duration and selective use of the recognisably limited number of functions that produce different outcomes. In terms of Miller's general principles, all groups fit into a theoretical system of greater generality and are governed by the same general principles. (1988, p. 34)

The problem with such approaches begins with a resolute effort on the part of authors like Douglas to aim at abstraction in an effort to deny the obviousness of the mess and diversity they confront. This is, among other things, a distinctively masculine approach and one that has been used frequently to claim prizes and fame for the level of abstractness which 'real' science and 'real' theory are said to manifest. Writers like Douglas seem to deny the obvious—namely, the simple fact that there are many different kinds of groups. Similarly, there are many different ways of working with groups, and we need to be clear about this diversity before we can go any further.

In Australia in the 1990s, there are many groups and many different styles of working with groups. We therefore need to reflect on the diversity of group work theories and practices. In this chapter we look at what are regarded as the traditional or mainstream forms of group work which have as their focus either various forms of social control or various forms of *therapy*. Both of these perspectives begin with the premise that some people—usually 'experts'—know what is best for other people. Group work, as shown in Chapter 2, has a history of being used by dominant groups to tell others what is wrong with them and/or how they should change. We suggest in Chapter 4 that, while group work can be used for social control or therapy, it can also be used to promote desirable forms of social change and social action.

Perspectives on group work

As a starting point for understanding group work, it is useful to consider a way of mapping some of the various approaches to working with groups. To keep the map simple we present three perspectives for developing that understanding of group work:

1 a remedial perspective;
2 a reciprocal perspective; and
3 a social goals perspective.

This chapter is about the first two perspectives. These perspectives do not describe the ways group work is done; rather, they describe some of the objectives associated with group work and capture some of the activities people engage in through groups. Each one of these perspectives is not necessarily restricted to specific professional or occupational settings—for instance, all three perspectives may be found in youth work, teaching or community work practice. Similarly, some of the recent trends in human resource development towards planning and managing through corporate learning (Senge

1990; Argyris 1990; Schon 1983) could also be defined as operating within the social goals perspectives.

We have further identified how these perspectives or orientations relate to some of the specific ways and places in which people work with groups:

Remedial orientation
• social control group work;
• therapeutic group work.

Reciprocal orientation
• Self-help and codependence groups;
• Organisational group work.

Social goals orientation
• community development group work;
• libratory group work;
• social action and social movement group work.

The remedial perspective

> The remedial perspective describes the orientation of group work designed to 'remedy' or to 'fix up' people's experience of distress, poverty or other problems. (These problems have often been defined by social workers, sociologists and counsellors as 'social dysfunction'.) The aim is to assist people to learn to do something which will 'fix' the problem. This is often attempted through specific behavioural or psychological changes.

The remedial perspective is often found in social work, counselling and therapeutic work. In youth work, for example, this approach may be practised in institutional settings dealing with juvenile justice, probation, drug rehabilitation, mental health and special education. This is a treatment or behaviour modification approach that is concerned with overcoming or changing 'problems' of a psychological, social or cultural nature through educational and developmental activities where the group is itself the means and the context for strengthening, treating, reforming or correcting the 'individual'. The remedial orientation is found in styles of group work such as social control group work and therapeutic group work.

Remedial perspective I: Social control group work

Social control group work is one of the oldest styles of group work around. It is a form of group work that begins with the assumption that there are right ways to behave or right things to think. It uses various group techniques to help people identified as 'deviant' learn how to behave in the 'right way' and/or to think the 'right thing'.

Social control group work sets up group processes so that group members can learn 'behaviours deemed appropriate to social inter-action. Few groups in this category have a pure education, pure socialisation, or a pure support orientation . . . [these ingredients are usually blended]'. (Brown 1991, p. 50)

Social control group work also rests on a *deficit theory*. Many education and welfare practices over the past century have relied on the assumption that particular people (like the poor or the unem-ployed) lack what the rest of us have, and that 'fixing' their per-ceived 'problems' means giving them what they lack. Sometimes what 'they' are said to lack is biological in origin—like intelligence. On other occasions, 'they' are said to lack training, appropriate values or the right behaviours—like a good diet, or budget-manage-ment skills.

Modern social control group work takes a group of people who are not behaving in 'socially appropriate ways' and establishes group processes that enable members to learn how to behave in 'appropri-ate ways'—that is, in ways that someone else has defined as normal and socially appropriate.

These groups use a variety of techniques to 're-socialise' or to re-educate people so as to force or encourage changes in attitude, aspirations, values or behaviour. Typically, this is justified on the grounds that when 'society' does not approve of someone else's beliefs or behaviours, that person (or group) is at fault and needs to be fixed or normalised. A simple example occurs when a school student begins to 'wag' school and becomes a 'truant'. It is usually assumed by most teachers and government officials that the problem lies neither with the school (that it is boring), nor with the teachers, but rather that the truant 'is' the problem. Typically the student is seen as 'having' a problem; he or she therefore needs to be re-socialised. There is something wrong with the student (or the student's family/community)—they have the problem and it is upon such a basis that interventions occur.

A considerable amount of this 'social control' group work depends on a set of theoretical views that also reflect modern 'common sense'. The theoretical tradition is called *structural func-tionalism* and has been very influential in North American sociology and social psychology textbooks. Structural functionalism has under-pinned and informed the traditional education and training of pro-fessional social workers, counsellors and group workers. It has to do with an account of 'society' and 'the individual' and how 'society' socialises 'individuals' into appropriate 'social roles'. 'Social roles', according to the functionalist viewpoint, are what people are forced or socialised into.

According to the social functionalist, a 'society' is a system of social relations in which members of that society agree on the most important things, like a set of beliefs and behaviours which makes up a moral consensus. Furthermore, this society is a system that normally tends to produce social order. Social order depends on the system being able to take new members of the society and socialise or educate the novices about how to behave, think and feel. This process (so it is claimed) is not chaotic or disordered, because it is organised around people learning how to fit into a variety of roles from the first days of their existence. A social role is a script similar to that given to an actor, which prescribes a set of behaviours about how to behave, feel and think. Such scripts provide details on what to do in roles like 'child', 'school pupil', 'mother', 'teacher', 'law-yer' or 'old woman'.

Social roles are defined as 'socially determined behaviours' that 'society' is said to design and allocate. Social control group work is about re-socialising or re-educating people into more 'appropriate' roles.

Most people, according to the functionalist sociological account, 'make it' by adjusting to the roles each of us is required to fulfil. Not everyone does make it, however. There are three kinds of people who signal that 'society' is not perfect. First, there are the *deviants*, who are identified as the ones who behave and think in ways that are different from what is established as normal. Second, there are the *delinquents* who are both different (not socialised properly) and who are also a bit bad (have a biological disposition towards anti-social behaviour). Finally, there are *criminals*, who are both different and very bad.

Each category or type represents the failure of socialisation processes. Given that families and schools are said to play a socialising role, they usually get the most blame for the failure to integrate. The usual response to such failures in our society ranges from placing 'them' into hospitals or schools to committing them to reformatories or prisons. The most extreme measure is capital punishment, but most modern societies prefer less overtly violent methods of 'correction' than killing or gaoling those who are simply different—the 'bad' and the 'mad'.

We have some difficulties with this account of 'society', 'social roles' and 'anti-social' behaviours—difficulties which became apparent when the following kinds of questions are asked. For a start, has any society ever existed that actually looked the way the functionalist account says it should—where there was moral consensus, where people were clear about the social boundaries, and where people conformed to social roles that functioned to maintain the whole system? Moreover, we may ask what 'socially appropriate behaviour' is? The structural functionalist perspective also raises issues about who is doing the defining of what is 'socially appropriate'—questions which relate to 'morality' and power.

Group work practice raises a number of fundamental issues about morality (or ethics) that often relate to why people do group work in the first place. (This does not exclusively refer to social control group work.) There are a number of problems with the story that 'societies' represent or are built out of a moral consensus:

1 We know that moral rules can change very quickly. Earlier this century in Australia, for example, opium was freely available at the local chemist shop. Now, however, the drug is illegal and the object of strong moral disapproval. Consider also the swiftness with which attitudes to cigarette smoking have changed over the past 20 years. Many other social practices have gone through the same process of change.
2 There are also difficulties with the supposed moral consensus about the multicultural nature of Australian society. There is no agreement about a number of quite important issues; furthermore, moral and attitudinal rules cannot be easily transported between cultures. Muslim groups generally outlaw the use of alcohol and some Muslim groups sanction practices which others find abhorrent—like female circumcision. Conversely, dominant Anglo-Australian practices of women revealing their near-naked bodies on beaches no doubt causes some Muslims considerable anguish.

Such differences rebut the simplistic claim that there is a wide-spread social consensus in Australia.

3 Moral rules are not always the subject of consensus within a society. It has, for example, been established by surveying people that 95 per cent believe it wrong to knowingly inflict pain and cruelty on another weaker human being. But does this mean that a moral consensus actually holds in practice in that society? What do we do when we also discover that large numbers of people actually do what they say should not be done? Stanley Milgram (1979) discovered that large numbers of people—more than 75 per cent of those studied—knowingly inflicted what they 'knew' to be pain on a vulnerable human being. When is a moral consensus really a consensus? Is it when many people say one thing but do another?

There is a place for some version of social control group work when there is a community concern about a social practice which is harmful. But it is not always easy to know what is harmful, or to work out when to intervene in other people's lives, let alone *how* to intervene. Some activities which cause trouble to other people ought to be addressed, and for these a group work approach would be at least as valuable as other approaches (e.g. gaol, drug treatment or admission to a psychiatric hospital)—and possibly more so. So while we should not take the story of anti-social behaviours as a simple matter of fact, especially when we consider the underlying reliance on moral arguments and claims, there are times and places when some activities need to be dealt with, and when group work may be a legitimate way of doing this.

For example, after 1945, many Australians discovered the pleasures (and pain) of owning mass-produced cars capable of high speeds. The result, when this was combined with alcohol, was an epidemic of road fatalities and injuries. By the 1980s, the police, the health care system, insurers, sections of the media and governments had had enough and instigated an expensive public awareness campaign, with the aim of instituting a new moral awareness about car use, speed, driving while tired and alcohol use. Moral opprobrium, shame and awareness were all used in an increasingly successful effort to stem the tide. These safe driving campaigns could be described as having a positive social value, even though in policy terms the impetus to do something came from a relatively small slice of 'Australian society'. Equally, many Australians would support a process of using group work with drivers convicted of drink driving, culpable driving and so on to force or encourage a process of greater responsibility on the road. In short, there are occasions when a case can be made for social control group work.

The issues of social consensus and 'anti-social' behaviour are complex, and we counsel caution. Before assuming that a particular activity or belief is 'anti-social' and requires remedial or corrective action, it is important to stop, think and reflect on what exactly is being said. If a case can be made for seeing a certain activity or belief as a problem, then the intervention should proceed. Having made that initial judgment, a further decision to begin social control group work can be a viable component of such an intervention. However, it could also turn out to be a crude and useless exercise designed to uphold outmoded or irrational belief systems at the expense of certain people. This is especially likely if members of the group are marginalised in terms of access to basic resources (like food, clothing, shelter, political power and security). Groups which are often marginalised in these ways include some women, Aborigines, recently arrived immigrants and young people. For these people, social control group work all too frequently just adds insult to injury.

Remedial perspective II: Therapeutic group work

Therapeutic group work is another common style of group work with a remedial orientation. It is a form of group work where the attainment of personal change is the main purpose of the group's activities. It also has some relation to the social control group work we have just considered, although it has more expressive and creative potential for some people who are looking for freedom from pain or distress.

> Therapeutic group work has been defined as: a systematic process and activity designed to remedy, cure, abate some disease, disability or problem. (Baker 1987, p. 164)

Therapeutic group work received an impetus during and after World War II, especially in North America, through the activities of some eminent 'humanist' psychologists like Carl Rogers and Abraham Maslow (Bach 1954). Humanists can be distinguished from both 'depth' psychologists like Freud and his psychoanalytic method or Jung and his analysis, and the behaviourist tradition associated with B.F. Skinner. By the late 1940s, the use of T-Groups—later called encounter groups—was well established, with industry using them to train sensitive managers (Rogers 1969).

The use of groups for training managers and employees has continued apace. Likewise, the success of training groups using adjustment-oriented models from Adler, Maslow et al. sponsored the development of therapeutic groups, a phenomenon which has also expanded.

Therapeutic group work is generally found in forms of practice where there is a practitioner who is responsible for running the group—for example, a psychiatrist, a psychologist, counsellor or a medical practitioner. It can, in some instances, be found in a self-help context where a group of people get together because they share a particular problem or experience and have decided to use a group process to address that problem.

1 Therapeutic groups are designed to address, if not 'cure', emotional problems relating to anything from a loss of self-esteem or anxiety through to alcoholism or drug use. Therapeutic group work is intended to assist people in coming to terms with a particular trauma, like being the parent of a murder victim or being caught in a major catastrophe like an earthquake or cyclone, or it can be used to help deal with major depressions and psychoses. Typically these therapeutic groups are run by counsellors, psychologists or psychiatrists and are aimed at addressing and possibly helping the members of the group to resolve emotional or psychiatric distress or disease.

2 The emphasis in therapeutic group work is on sharing information and discussing the experiences of being mad or upset or depressed or hurt. Sometimes these groups use a particular technique like psycho-drama or role-playing to assist the group members to gain insight into a problem or experience. The point of sharing information and experiences is to develop an understanding of what is common, partly to understand the issues and problems and to begin to resolve the problem. Many of these therapeutic groups are established inside community health settings, in outpatient clinics and inside psychiatric hospitals and medical clinics.

In modified ways, they can also be used in self-help settings of the type that movements like Alcoholics Anonymous have used for decades. Or they can be used to help men who have abused their partners and want to resolve their anger and control their tempers.

3 Therapeutic group work can also address issues in relationships (like parent–child or husband–wife problems). These might involve, for example, the use of groups run by professionals who want to help people be more effective parents and who offer a diversity of what are called 'helping skills' in sessions for Parent Effectiveness Training. Often, marriage guidance counselling can be seen as a special kind of group work process using a counsellor and the two partners as the group. There is also the special therapeutic group called the family therapy group.

These family therapy sessions are run by counsellors specialising in the field. These professionals take one of the more powerful and most common of naturally occurring groups, 'the family', and attempt to uncover the dynamics of understandings, political processes and other factors that are causing one or more members of the family to experience a problem or distress. The objective usually involves finding solutions that the family as a whole can think about and act upon.

Another possible group may consist of adolescents addressing issues of concern arising from living inside a particular family or household. Again, the idea here is for group members to share ideas and experiences, to develop support for each other and to try to develop solutions to particular issues. That is, the members of the group use the group as a resource to test ideas, establish that others are dealing with the same issues and together try to develop some answers.

We have similar reservations in this situation to those we expressed above about social control orientations. One concern is the tendency within therapeutic groups to dress up what are often social and moral issues in the language of medicine and science. What, for example, are we to make of claims like, 'The extent to which the group can be mobilised to offer mutual aid will often be the determining factor in motivating group members to give up unhealthy or unproductive behaviours' (Brown 1991, p. 48)?

Words like 'healthy behaviours' or 'unhealthy relations' imply medical categories and knowledge. But scientific-sounding language can be used to cover up what are really moral opinions—judgments that really say 'I do like' or 'I approve' of this person or of that particular behaviour; or alternately, 'I don't like this person' or 'I don't approve of that person's behaviour'. The use of medical metaphors help to legitimise and give greater standing to 'diagnosis' of the problem by making the assessment sound scientific and objective. Medical metaphors, however, often muddy the issues and deflect attention away from the social, political and moral assumptions underlying the problems at hand.

In the twentieth century, there are many more people than before who are prepared to criticise other people's behaviours and dispositions—whether they relate to eating, exercising, using drugs, sexual activity or religious activity. Again, it is not always easy to establish whether this growth in professional observation and critique is a good or wise thing.

Take the case of one of the great pioneers of 'depth' psychology—Sigmund Freud. Freud lived with a number of his own quite 'unhealthy' behaviours, including habitual cigar smoking which probably killed him, agoraphobia (now classified as a compulsive obsessive disorder) and his need to always arrive three hours early at the railway station. Freud also understood that a cure for these behaviours was not possible and that at best his patients could gain insights into their pain and distress. Alternately, Freud also understood that if a particular pain was resolved, this may occur at a considerable cost. Treating the great composer Mahler in 1905, Freud offered to end Mahler's painful, even depressive, preoccupation with death, but at the cost of curtailing his creative work. Mahler wisely did not pursue therapy.

The point being made here is a simple one: what is 'unhealthy' for one person can be healthy or productive for another. For example, William Burroughs, an American writer, has maintained a lifelong heroin habit into the 1990s as part of his creative commitment to literature. Balzac, the great nineteenth century French novelist, drank 40 to 50 cups of strong coffee a day to maintain his demanding schedule of writing a novel every two weeks! This habit killed him by enlarging his heart to the point that he suffocated himself to death.

The category 'healthy'—or 'unhealthy'—can be used by people to express a degree of moral disapproval about an activity or disposition they do not like. Masturbation and coffee drinking are activities that for centuries attracted accusations of being 'unhealthy'. Conversely, cigarette smoking was for a long time seen as not being a problem and into the 1950s some Australian doctors even 'prescribed' cigarettes as a treatment for people who were 'nervy'. The language of 'health' can be used to compel people into decisions they may not ordinarily wish to make or which may even damage them.

If a person is convinced that there is a problem, or that they 'have' a problem, then that could be enough to warrant some kind of therapeutic intervention, but this is not an absolute warrant. If we can justify going on because we think a good case can be made for seeing a certain activity or belief as a problem, then we should proceed. Clarifying the answers to these types of questions is important as a prerequisite for working out whether therapeutic group work is called for.

The reciprocal perspective

The *reciprocal perspective* in group work is about the development of a mutual aid system where people come together to identify some common problem/s and to develop some solutions to those problem/s. Early examples of the reciprocal approach in the nineteenth century included the establishment of mutual aid organisations like the trade union movement and health and medical insurance societies like Hospital Benefits Association.

In the twentieth century, there have been many examples of the reciprocal perspective like the self-help organisation now popularly known as Alcoholics Anonymous. The reciprocal perspective is also found now in a variety of recreational work, as well as with a number of community work approaches to health, environmental and local government issues. The reciprocal approach also has a lot to do with self-help approaches where activities that once were informal and a 'natural' part of family and community life have taken on more of an institutional and organisational character.

The reciprocal perspective is a transitional orientation that bridges between the remedial perspective and the social goals perspective. It is transitional because at one end of the spectrum it can involve approaches to fixing identifiable problems of individual people—such as those dealt with by Alcoholics Anonymous—and at the other end of the spectrum it can take on a social change perspective—as in the case of the union movement.

The reciprocal perspective establishes certain tensions around the role of the professional group worker. While the remedial model typically has a therapist/worker as an initiator and facilitator, the self-help group relies on people who have a problem or an issue working together within a reciprocal framework. They may have (although they do not necessarily need) a group work facilitator. Where this is the case, the facilitator often uses ideas that originated from within the group. An example of this in the youth field is friends who share their experiences being used as a means of introducing peer-education programs in areas of health—particularly in relation to diseases like HIV—the use of certain drugs including cigarette smoking and alcohol, and the adoption of sensible birth-control practices.

Facilitating groups in the reciprocal perspective

The group work facilitator working in a reciprocal perspective usually pays attention to the following kinds of tasks:

- helping group members to clarify the point and purpose of the group;
- paying attention to helping members to clarify their thoughts and feelings about the process (e.g. what they feel about being forced to participate if they have had no choice);
- helping members to access information that may be useful in solving an organisational problem for which the group has been set up;
- assisting the group to develop its own solutions. These solutions can be generated in a variety of ways, including the use of brainstorming techniques that use large sheets of paper and whiteboards to record a variety of possible approaches to a problem. Generally, group members will be encouraged to generate as many ideas as possible. As mentioned, a 'brainstorming' session is a useful way to begin to overcome some of the difficulties the group has. Moreover, getting people to 'own' a common problem or a particular situation in a non-threatening way is a valuable skill for the facilitator to have.

Organisational group work

The reciprocal perspective can also be found in organisations. There the reciprocal model has been developed and applied by organisational development practitioners to develop personnel training or to help solve organisational issues inside companies.

Organisational group work is about using groups and group processes inside an organisation to achieve some goal or objective that people who work in that organisation want to achieve. In the 1990s, organisational group work involves using small groups to assist people who are working in the same workplace to work together with greater harmony and more effectively in rapidly changing and often difficult work environments.

Attaining waged work in the 1990s is more difficult for many people for a number of reasons. The advent of new technologies, a series of economic recessions since the mid-1970s, the threat of unemployment, falling wages in some industries, and economic and managerial restructuring have caused many aspects of our lives to change in significant ways. Many of these changes have altered the ways in which people work, and in some instances the changes have meant the threat of unemployment or under-employment. For many people, this context of transformation creates considerable uncertainty and stress.

Some managers and administrators in organisations have come to see the small work group as an important unit in the organisational structure. The team or group can provide experience and 'know-how' about the work of the organisation. The group can apply this 'know-how' to improving its own and the organisation's effectiveness. The development of learning groups, where time is given for members to talk through the possible ways of improving their work practices, has become a powerful tool for assisting organisations to meet the challenges of workplace reform with minimum job losses. Using a *reciprocal approach* to organisational group work can improve the effectiveness of people who are working to achieve common goals, cope with change and improve the quality of their work practices and output.

In a similar way to community development group work, organisational group work is task-focused. However, the basis of being a member of this kind of group, the degree of freedom enjoyed by members, and the setting of agendas and objectives are likely to be more constrained by power relations which are operating within a work organisation, especially where there are the 'normal' power inequalities between employers/managers on the one hand and employees/volunteers on the other.

The styles of organisational group work are usually determined by the nature of the organisation. In spite of the contemporary managerialist rhetoric, private-sector companies work in quite different ways from community agencies and government departments. The culture is usually different, social relations are often diverse and the missions are different. Things like attitudes to women workers, the scale of the organisation, the commitment to values or motivations like equity versus profit, the intellectual and political demands on workers, and the role of volunteers (if any), all impact on the kind of group work that gets done. If you work in a women's refuge referral centre, the kind of group work you are likely to encounter will be quite different from the kind of group work likely to be found in a major multinational banking company, or in a medium-scale government agency.

Other differences between organisational groups include:

1 The group may meet a few times, or it may go on for a long time.
2 Group members may be volunteers, or they may have no choice about their membership.
3 Members could be ambivalent about being in the group, or there may be a lot of enthusiasm. Whether, for example, the group meets during the working day or meets outside normal work hours may impact on people's perceptions of the process and their feelings about being there.

The purpose of the group

When the organisational issues are difficult, a group process is often seen as the only or the best way to solve a problem—for example, when there is a big problem between a manager and his or her staff, or when there are budget problems and solutions need to be found.

Sometimes an organisation needs to review itself and its mission or strategy and a group process can be the best way of doing this. There may be a major restructuring taking place within the organisations that is bringing together units of the organisation that have not previously worked together, or there may be a history of bad relationships between workers. In such cases, senior managers may hire a consultant to run a series of problem-solving workshops or groups to try to assist in resolving the issues. These initiatives can work well or can turn out to be absolute disasters.

Political fighting within organisations can be at least as fierce and difficult as the political fighting found in community development groups. In Australia in the 1990s, organisational politics often have a distinct gendered quality as men and women contest various definitions of what is 'right behaviour' or 'good policy' regarding issues such as the quality of social work relations, or promotion and employment practices. Or there may be significant differences about what are acceptable attitudes and behaviours at work.

Organisational group work is also constrained by the scale of the organisation. Working inside a small community health centre with a total of seven staff is very different to working inside a large agency with a hundred or more workers, or a major government department, or a big multinational corporation with tens of thousands of workers.

The group facilitator may be a line manager, or a senior member of the organisation, or a volunteer selected from within the group, or simply someone who is regarded as having a special set of competencies in group work, or he or she could be a highly paid consultant brought in from outside to sponsor or oversee a process of organisational change. The group processes used in organisational group work usually includes a range of tasks. These are managed or facilitated by an experienced group work facilitator.

Organisational group work as learning

It is important to develop a positive culture inside today's 'anxious organisation'. The increasing awareness by many educators, trainers and administrators about the positive value of cooperation rather than competition has led to the development of a significant body of literature and group of practices for collaborative decision-making, the development of work teams and 'total quality management' within the workplace. Group facilitators can assist if they help group members to identify and value diversity, develop common objectives that relate to their work and cooperate in establishing better ways of working together. These are the basic elements of collaborative learning. Seen in this way, and given a supportive working culture, big changes in workplaces can provide opportunities for workers to increase the satisfaction they get from the organisation, as well as their contribution to it. If this is to work effectively, structures, administrative procedures, roles and responsibilities need to be different from those usually associated with the traditional workplace.

A major obstacle to change—whether in social relations, in

organisations or in oneself—is a sense of powerlessness or a loss of agency. The feeling of having no agency is often experienced by people when they face too much change, fear the unknown, or when there is an unequal exercise of power. Many workers experience and fear a loss of agency, insecurity and a loss of face when undergoing major workplace changes. Fear of change in the workplace is often powerful because it may mean the loss of a job, income and status.

Things to do

1 It is important to begin by identifying and then removing inse-curity and uncertainty about employment. The tendency for some managers is to resist change because they think that change reduces their control over the situation in which they work.
2 Create a climate where 'weakness' or limitations become oppor-tunities for devising new ways of doing things, rather than an opportunity for condemnation and negative sanctioning. Organisations that are genuinely committed to improving the performance of their business or service provide a context and the security required for effective group work practices.
3 Develop a guarantee of security that will promote frank and open discussion, and facilitate and develop relationships within the organisation that are directed towards establishing and maintain-ing collaborative and cooperative work practices.

Introducing what we see as positive changes requires processes that are directed towards equalising traditional power imbalances inside organisations between managers and workers. Strategies which follow the approach identified earlier as the reciprocal model can increase both personal and group autonomy.

Participatory decision-making is one way of equalising power that is rarely used in many organisations. It is also a strategy for allowing people to be informed about what is happening, and to 'own' the new directions, policies and practices that are set in place.

Action learning

One approach which aligns the activities of the organisation with the learning experiences of the individual worker is known as action learning. Organisations that follow this practice are referred to as *learning organisations*. Peter Senge is one management theorist who has pushed the idea that companies which harness the benefits of organisational learning improve their overall performance. His book, *The Fifth Discipline: The Art and Practice of the Learning Organisation,* has made Senge and the term 'action learning' quite famous.

Many organisations, large and small, from the private and the public sector, have adopted these ideas. Recently there has also been a proliferation of business consultancies, designed to assist organisations in the change-over from more traditional management structures. This change-over involves introducing 'total quality improvement strategies', and helping workers to deal with changing contexts and/or the internationalisation of their operations. Increasingly, these consultants use group work approaches to working with small groups of employees in these organisations. They also encourage a more participative, democratic and collaborative organisational climate.

The assumption of many consultants working to develop a learning organisation is that every group and person has the capacity for affecting personal change and overall organisational improvement and change. Most facilitators who use the reciprocal perspective also operate on the assumption that collective group action can develop individual self-determination through which positive social change can occur. In the workplace, this is translated into personal learning for organisational improvement and change.

The process has been so effective with workers at all levels that it is now being adapted to provide specialist training and development for managers. This is because, above all else, good management needs be about working harmoniously with people. This requires a degree of maturity, sensitivity and self-awareness that many managers just do not have. Managers who are accustomed to operating in authoritarian, hierarchical ways do not make good group members. This is why there is a need for such people to improve their self-awareness and develop new skills and understandings in order to foster genuinely cooperative, pleasant and democratic work practices.

One of the most effective forums for enhancing self-awareness is the small learning group. Four to eight managers who commit themselves to working together for a set period of time can provide unrivalled learning experiences for each other. Such learning groups are comprised of managers who share similar levels of responsibility, but who come from different organisations.

They can provide feedback to each other as well as opportunities for comparison that are seen as credible. These groups work together on developing strategies for their respective workplaces. And, in the process of problem solving, they can improve their awareness as members of a team. For many members, these collaborative settings also mean they can afford to take risks. Risk-taking and experimentation can help learning—particularly when they are accompanied by immediate, sensitive and credible feedback. Participants return to their organisations with a better self-understanding and ability to deal with the changes they are implementing.

When workers adopt the practices of the *learning organisation philosophy*, they usually employ those who are skilled at working with small groups to facilitate processes of mutual learning. These are group facilitators capable of convincing participants of the value of pooling collective knowledge for the purpose of creating innovative change.

Small groups in large workplaces help humanise work experiences and, ideally, allow everyone the opportunity, and provide them with the encouragement, to contribute directly and visibly to the development of that workplace. In a small way, they can begin to democratise our workplaces.

Review questions

1 What are the main ways of working with groups identified in this chapter?
2 Do you think the distinctions between the main types of group work are watertight? Explain why you think they are—or are not.
3 Do definitions of group work really matter, and if so, why?
4 What do *you* think about the two perspectives on doing group work—the remedial and reciprocal perspectives—discussed in this chapter?

4

The social goals perspective for working with groups

Introduction

Working with groups can provide opportunities for participants to set their own goals, learn through the achievement of those goals, and pursue social change. This is the *social goals perspective* on group work. As we indicated in the Introduction, our preference is for those kinds of group work that are directed towards promoting democratic and progressive social change, and which enhance people's agency while respecting the differences related to their identity.

A social goals approach to group work recognises that people bring to the group a diverse range of experiences, values and expectations. Using a social goals perspective in working with groups means that activities are designed so that the person's agency is enhanced through his or her participation in the group. It is a style of practice that not only accommodates difference, but also enhances personal understanding, tolerance and inclusive decision-making.

Social goals perspective

The social goals perspective is so named because it uses group work to bring about social change. It has an explicit objective of using group work to produce change on a larger scale than the other two perspectives.

> The social goals perspective in group work is a progressive political exercise directed towards the development of new forms of social consciousness and action. There is also an assumption held by many of those in the group that they have a social responsibility and will try to promote some form of social change.

The social goals perspective is about developmental and social change approaches to group work. This approach is often observed in groups operating with explicit political goals or which are working towards social change and social action. Underlying the social goals model is a close relationship between *collective action* and *personal agency*. This perspective presupposes that all people are capable of self-determination and can make sense of their life situations in order to initiate and influence events in the world around them.

Typically, those working within a social goals perspective consider every group and their members to be capable of personal and social change. The worker or group facilitator reveals that capacity in the group, then resources group members to bring about change through social action. The idea of people learning and developing through their associations in groups has led many teachers to see the value of such group work practices in their own work and to set structured learning experiences through specific group processes. Another feature of the social goals approach to group work is that the type of collective action it requires helps develop personal and social competencies.

Some core characteristics of the social goals model should be spelt out before we look at specific examples.

Features of the social goals perspective

1 *Self-determination or agency*—It is helpful for good group work practice if the people involved in the activities believe in the benefits of positive change, because it is they who make the change.

2 *Participation*—Social goals-oriented group work involves people having a *sense of belonging* to a particular group. It

is also important that they are appreciated by other members of the group. Believing that a group's activities are worthwhile and that one's contribution to those activities is valued by others encourages further learning, commitment and action.

3 *Communication*—Participation and democratic decision-making require communication that is honest, sensitive and open.

4 *Acceptance and tolerance of difference*—The idea that each group member is of value, regardless of age, gender, or station in life, assists in group work practice. Good group work practice involves making the time and place to identify each member's attributes.

5 *Reciprocity*—Opportunities for making contributions and receiving benefits from group membership are an important aspect of group work that affirms members.

6 *Equality*—Recognition that we can all learn from one another fosters effective group work. This recognition is also an admission or acceptance of some degree of equality. It is a position that is quite different from elitist notions that one person or a small elite knows what is best for the entire group and that those who know have little or no time for the views of others, who they regard as either ignorant or wrong. It is important to recognise the value of everybody's potential contribution to each other and to the group.

There are a number of good examples of group work oriented to a social goals model. The first is the kind of group work done by community development workers.

The social goals perspective 1: Community development group work

The primary purpose of groups involved in community development usually relates to political action and social change towards expanding the sphere of democracy and citizenship in practical ways. Community development group work is about planning strategy and initiating action, often over a long period, to improve people's access to resources or justice in ways which merit the use of the idea of citizenship and citizens' rights.

Community development is also often about developing bonds between people for the purpose of cooperative action. It is concerned with community members influencing decisions that affect their lives. It is also about community members increasing their access to resources. Community development means people working collectively rather than as independent individuals. Community development workers use their knowledge of group dynamics and group work to increase the effectiveness of the activities of those they work with. A primary function of community work is bringing groups of people together to work collectively, to achieve common objectives and a sense of their own power and competence. In this way, a number of similarities between community development and other forms of group work in the settings already mentioned become evident. Within the community development setting however, little else is predetermined.

Community development group work

Community development group work is a form of group work that is oriented to practical social action and change. Typically, the group has a strong task focus; its members want to do something quite specific. This kind of group work uses group processes and the resources of a group to fight for a desired change in the life of those members of the group and sometimes in the wider community. It may be designed to manage some aspect of a local community's resources better, or it may be working at a larger level as part of a broader national or even global network level for change around some issue of justice or equity.

For example, parents may be fighting to save a local school or library facing closure by a cost-cutting government. It may be about a group of young mothers in an outlying suburb, with few services, wanting to open a kindergarten or develop a public transport service. Community development group work may involve a group of young people with a strong environmental commitment who want to save a local forest from woodchippers. Or it may be a whole locality facing the shutdown of a major industry that has provided the *raison d'être* for the community.

- Community development group work involves using groups for many different purposes.
- It can involve using group processes for planning to produce press releases; or it can involve designing a demonstration, or planning a rally, liaising with police and governments and media.
- It may involve a group process for designing and carrying out a piece of survey research and analysing the data—perhaps to demonstrate that a local community wants a football oval.
- It may mean members of a group liaising with other community groups and building up and maintaining strong links with other professionals, community health centres or political groups.
- It may involve the use of group processes for raising money, managing complex organisational structures and developing a budget system. It can also include setting up a paid position and employing someone to fill that position and then managing the staff employed.

Community development group work can be done in most places. Often it is sponsored within an already existing and funded community agency like a community health centre, a neighbourhood house or centre, or a women's refuge. Sometimes it is supported by federal or state government funding and there is an obligation to account for the program and its spending to some government agency. At times the problem or the target of a community development group is a government action or policy. (The use of state-sponsored programs or agencies to run an anti-state project can create problems and tensions, for obvious reasons.) Sometimes the objective is to get government to spend money on a new project or on an expanded service, in which case it becomes a matter of winning friends amongst, and influencing, members of the government and public service personnel.

Sometimes community development group work takes the form of a *social movement*, like the Peace, Green or Women's movements. As we continue to cut down forests, move private dwellings to make way for freeways, or sell off public or community assets like electricity or water resources in various parts of Australia, we will continue to see spontaneous forms of community work and community group work emerge.

Sometimes the community development group can be self-managing and develop leadership and organisation from within. Often there is a local community development worker who can play a small or a large role in leading and/or supporting the group. The community worker will do what they can to mobilise the resources of the group to use its abilities and its capacities to achieve the group's objectives. At times, as the group process unfolds, the group discovers that the initial objective is too big or that it will take too long and a process of renegotiation of the objectives takes place. On the other hand, the group may make the opposite discovery and find that its initial sense of purpose is too limited. Here the community worker can play a useful role in reshaping the objectives. An experienced, receptive and sensitive community worker can be a major resource, offering support, recognising discouragements, developing skills and celebrating triumphs. The community group worker's role is similar to being a successful coach in a netball, Australian Rules football or Rugby team.

Community development group work is not about discovering long-buried emotional pains and fantasies of group members, nor is it about massaging emotional pains back from where they came. Emotional experiences can and will take place and will need to be dealt with as they emerge—people's feelings certainly have an impact, even in community development group work, and they can make quite a difference, especially in a highly politicised contest for a new kindergarten or in struggles opposing a freeway development. But experiencing and dealing with feelings is not the primary point of the group's work.

In terms of community development group work, the leader (or facilitator or coordinator) has a number of main tasks.

Community development tasks

Some of the tasks community development workers address are as follows.

- A common cause or consensus is established among those who are part of the group.
- The group facilitator sets out explicitly to work coopera-

tively with groups. This will involve setting common goals and increasing the competence and confidence of the group members.

- Community group work is also directed towards consciousness-raising. This involves drawing on people's experiences and life histories, with a view to identifying key experiences of powerlessness (or of being powerful) to see what can be learned about these experiences. It is through sharing common experiences that community members come to see their situation in relation to socioeconomic and political institutional practice and arrangements.

- The community group worker is there to help the group plan for concerted action. Unlike some other group work, being in a group is not the end of the process. A lot of community group work is about taking action outside the group in other forums, so as to get something done. Being in a group is often the means to another end.

- Community development work may also be about working out what went well and what did not work. This involves the use of evaluation techniques and today the community development worker may have to involve all members in evaluation and accountability procedures.

- Effective community group workers will often want to recognise indigenous leadership and hand over their role to someone from the community. Working out how to do this, who to do it with and when to do it can all take a lot of skill and art.

- More generally, community group work can also play a large part in transferring skills and responsibilities to the group as a whole.

Outcomes of effective community development group work

Belonging to such a group can enable individuals to feel:

- *Competent*—Everybody has skills of some kind and appreciates having their attributes affirmed; this affirmation also promotes confidence.
- *Valued*—When we feel our contribution is appreciated by others, we tend to value ourselves more.

- *Knowledgeable*—When people feel that their contribution is relevant to the task and moves the discussion/task along, members tend to feel knowledgeable.

Those developing a social goals perspective in group work identify the potential for social change. The worker responds to the developments of the group and, through social action objectives:

- assists the group in identifying the problems, issues and objectives that members consider provide the group's purpose and direction;
- resources group members for an exploration of possible avenues for inter-group action with other interested people and groups;
- contributes to the development of community activities which gain acceptance for the group's endeavours;
- encourages group involvement in services and programs that can expand their options for achieving wider social goals;
- cultivates the social consciousness of groups for the purpose of enhancing the political and social awareness of group members;
- transfers the leadership of the group from worker to group members.

Community development group work is a form of group work with strong political and 'public' qualities to it.

Social goals perspective 2: Conscientisation or liberatory group work

The final broad kind of group work process that we are interested in here concerns the use of group work to engage in a process of freeing people who are caught in oppressive social relations and settings.

Many Australians may feel they do not need to know about or do anything that looks like liberatory group work because we are all free and equal in Australia and oppression and inequality is something only foreigners suffer. This view has become prominent in the 1980s and 1990s as governments and the major political parties, along with key elements of the Australian media, claim that what 'really matters' is the individual getting out there into the marketplace, competing and battling away in the jungle of life. George Wills (1995) explained the current distribution of wealth and income in Australia, which is unequal, as the result of the unequal distribution of marketable skills of individuals.

This is a fashionable view; it is, however, inaccurate. (Whatever happened to inheritance, which explains 80 per cent of the current distribution of wealth in Australia?) Many Aboriginal people, many women, gays and lesbians, long-term unemployed people and homeless people know that having or not having marketable skills does not explain why they are living in poverty, why they experience oppression, or why they are disadvantaged. In terms of unemployment, we could have everyone working for a PhD over the next few years, but this would not mean they would have a job after they graduated. Unemployment, poverty, poor health, oppression, violence and lack of advantage result from many complex patterns, including the distribution of capital and wealth, power relations, who controls the flow of 'information' and who chooses what gets to be counted as information. Added to this is an array of attitudes and stereotypes otherwise identified as ageism, racism, sexism, homophobia and religious fundamentalism, all of which help to shape people's lives and opportunities—or the lack of them.

Paulo Friere

It was this kind of thinking which influenced a Brazilian Marxist and Jesuit priest named Paulo Friere in the 1960s. Friere's early work took place in the context of the rise in Latin America of a branch of Catholic theology called Liberation Theology. Liberation Theology was produced out of extreme poverty, the excesses of right-wing military governments and Marxism. It may look odd to Australian eyes, especially local Catholics, but this mix (of poverty, right-wing militarism and Marxism) has produced interesting forms of social action and community development.

Friere began his work in Brazil under military junta auspices in 1967. The Brazilian government wanted a literacy program taught to peasants in a remote part of Brazil. The government presumably wanted a minimal literacy program to enable peasants to read the government-controlled press. Friere, who was a professor of education at a Sao Paulo university, seized the opportunity to put in place a program of literacy. The idea was simple: he wanted to let illiterate peasants experience the power of being able to name the world as they experienced and saw it, and not as dictated by textbooks written by people who were a long way from them and their communities.

Using simple group processes, illiterate peasants quickly named and renamed what they thought were the important things around them.

Friere encouraged peasants to name the social world and its social relations between 'men' and 'women', 'children' and 'parents', and then to name the relations between 'peasants', 'landlords' and absent 'landholders', which were then described as 'oppressive' and 'greedy'. The peasants began to develop a vocabulary that was at once political, ethical and liberatory. Once they gained the power to name their social world and could write about it, they also began thinking about their experiences of oppression and exploitation. The peasants began to do what many would have done if they had the same opportunity: they began to challenge the relationships between the peasants and landlords and tried to change them. Everywhere Friere's teachers went, they left behind empowered peasant communities who demanded social justice and who experienced themselves as free, rational and competent people.

Friere's work (which he has written about in a number of books) is an inspiring story of how ordinary people can begin to transform their world. It is not immediately clear how the logic of the Freierean work can be applied to a place like Australia, where the job of producing literacy is mainly one concerning the schools, governments and experts who may not appreciate, or approve of, Friere's work. Yet Friere's work has been studied and debated, and aspects of it have been applied by many social movements. It has been applied to parts of the Women's Movement, which used the *consciousness-raising group* as a way of understanding the experiences of those women who felt exploited and oppressed. Friere's work has also been used for *mobilising* the insights and understanding of this as part of a process of *empowering* women.

It is hard to characterise the *type* of group work which social movements like the Women's Movement have traditionally used, because such movements have used combinations of therapeutic group work and community development group work with a particular commitment to learning processes. The Women's Movement, like many other organisations, has certainly used the group as a place where people tell their stories and clarify the meaning of their own experiences. In these consciousness-raising groups, people can address personal pains and aspirations, while allowing people to see that others have gone through the same or similar experiences.

Consciousness-raising can be regarded as a special form of learning that is about becoming free and empowered. Leaving the group process to simply 'consciousness raise' may be therapeutically useful, but for many women it has not been enough. The point, as one famous misogynist philosopher and failed revolutionary called Karl Marx put it, is not merely to interpret the world, but to change it. Consciousness-raising groups also share some features of the community development approach, since they stress the use of group processes as ways to get things done, like planning a strategy of change, carrying out a political strategy, developing an advertising process, bringing the press into a campaign, lobbying politicians, and/or staging a demonstration.

The work of Friere might sound like it is a long way away from Australians in the 1990s—most of whom live in suburbs. To bring the point closer to home, let us look at a famous and still current experiment in social change called the Family Centre Project.

The Family Centre Project—the Brotherhood of St Laurence

In 1933, an Anglican priest named Father Gerard Kennedy Tucker came from Sydney to Fitzroy to found a small religious group called the Brotherhood of St Laurence. The Brotherhood gathered together religious people who had a commitment to social justice and who wanted to work among the poor. It was at the height of the Great Depression, and Tucker became a major figure in Melbourne as he fought for social justice. Through the 1930s, the Brotherhood fought against slum housing, poverty and unemployment.

In 1972, this Melbourne-based welfare agency closed its traditional welfare bureau and embarked on an experimental program that was designed to test new ways of working with low income families. The program which began in 1973 became known as the Family Centre Program. The new practice—wisdom that emerged from the Family Centre Project—influenced welfare practice in Victoria and Australia generally. Information about the Family Centre Program was disseminated through research, evaluation reports and regular progress reports. These publications and the experiences they reported on challenged contemporary welfare practice.

The Family Centre Project was designed to achieve social change using participatory strategies to increase power over their life decisions for a group of low-income families. It included a guaranteed minimum income paid weekly by the Brotherhood to each family, as well as access to financial grants for the improvement of their housing, health and training. The project was situated in a multi-purpose building in Fitzroy, an inner city suburb of Melbourne. The area was well serviced by public housing, welfare agencies and public transport. A multi-disciplinary staff was employed and the project commenced with a guaranteed three-year duration (later extended to six years).

The staff of the project followed a developmental model of practice that was designed to achieve a social change objective using participatory strategies. Some of the core objectives of the project are summarised below.

The Family Centre Project model

Goal

To improve the socioeconomic functioning of certain low-income 'multi-problem' families.

Process

To develop participative strategies to assist the members develop power over:

- resources;
- relationships;
- information; and
- decision-making.

In the Brotherhood project, the factors used to develop and maintain individual and family agency took account of the four kinds of power listed above. In each case, the 'theory' of empowerment underpinning the project was that if people could get some control over these four aspects of their lives, their agency would be enhanced.

1 *Resources*—The core resources included a certain level of income that came as a form of a guaranteed minimum income. This was paid weekly to each of the participating families. There were also financial grants to improve housing, health and training of the families, access to a multi-disciplinary staff and access to a multi-purpose building. It also helped that the families knew the project was guaranteed to run for six years.

2 *Relationships*—One feature of this project was the belief that if people felt they had the ability to shape the relationships that were important to them, then their capacity to act and make those improvements developed. Among the changes introduced were new methods of work used by staff that ensured cooperation, equality and accountability of staff to those previously defined as 'clients' with all of the dependency that term connotes.

3 *Information*—It became apparent, as the project got underway, that people also needed to have certain information if they were to act freely and responsibly. People needed access to the information that was valuable to them and this directly affected their lives. The project therefore emphasised the need for programs that increased the level of the participants' awareness of the socioeconomic structures that restricted and oppressed them. This also involved responding to those forces in ways that reduced their influence on individuals, families and the community.

4 *Decision-making*—Finally, families involved in the project were to be empowered to make their own decisions. Agency is about the capacity to make decisions. Opportunities were structured for participants to play an active role in developing not only their personal life plans, but also the project itself and community social change.

These four powers needed to be achieved in sequence:

1 power over resources in order to establish the potential of mobility;
2 power over relationships to establish faith in one's own ability to act;
3 power over information to establish understanding and objectives.
4 It only became possible to act—that is, to make decisions—if these above three requirements were met.

The aspect of this project that is of most interest to us is the style of group work practice used by the workers. Traditionally the Brotherhood's welfare service had been staffed by social workers and welfare workers, who operated with their 'clients'—defined as people with deficits—and who used traditional casework methods. The Family Centre not only brought together other workers, like youth workers and teachers from the Department of Youth and Children's Services, but it was also committed to developing new approaches to its work.

Group work in the Brotherhood of St Laurence project

One of the project's basic objectives was to 'challenge' the 'deficit therapeutic approach'. Rather than seeing a fault or lack of something in the family, or within individual people, that required a traditional social work/casework approach, the idea behind the project was to work *with* the family members and to develop a resourcing and participative approach. The literature that emerged describing the project identified the style and practice of this approach in terms of a *developmental model*. It was designed to emphasise cooperation, more equality and much more accountability of paid staff to the people in the project hitherto defined as clients— a *social goals* approach.

The developmental model worked when dealing with people on a one-to-one basis. It also worked when dealing with Family Centre members in small and large groups. There were also many styles of working within groups that included camping experiences, shopping expeditions, discussion groups and cooperative meal preparation.

One of the important ways in which opportunities were provided for participants to play an active role in the development of the project itself was through the institution of a democratically elected committee of family members. The introduction of this innovation was later described (Liffman 1978, p. 64):

> In March 1973, only four months after the project had commenced, one family member suggested to staff that the families should help run the centre through some sort of committee. After discussion among staff, this suggestion was taken up with considerable alacrity and a chain of events was set in motion that had within a month culminated in the calling of a meeting of all families to elect a committee of management.

The committee of eight family members (four men and four women), one representative of the large number of volunteers involved in the project and one paid staff member was elected by all involved in the project. The introduction of this initiative was seen by the staff as crucial to the achievement of the participatory objectives of the project. The staff believed that it was important that the project develop genuine participation by the family members in final decision-making. The creation of appropriate structures clearly directed to this end was necessary.

The achievement by the families of true power over decision-making came to be seen not only as a test of the feasibility of the project's assumptions and objectives, but also, a little wistfully perhaps, as providing families with an awareness, confidence and skills that could enable them to participate in a larger community context. (Liffman 1978, p. 65)

From its inception, the Management Committee was credited by staff with an important educational role:

. . . the committee would provide the centre's members with the opportunity to learn from experience the techniques of rational group decision-making, discussion and representation, to improve their skills and confidence, and to develop an understanding of the issues involved in the operation of the Family Centre Project. (Liffman 1978, p. 66)

The staff member who became the first staff representative on the committee was a person with considerable experience and skills in group work. His role was a complex one. He facilitated the group process, provided guidance in meeting procedure and supported the Family Centre members in this new experience of participation, decision-making and the exercise of authority. For example, the basic procedures of committee processes all had to be learnt from scratch—by people for whom this was the first taste ever of the opportunity to participate in any organised decision-making body.

There were innumerable dramas and crises in the lives of these early committees. Basic issues of personality, status, accomplishment, relationships, identity and the exercise of power were all being experienced for the first time in the semi-public arena of the group. There were walkouts, angry shouting matches and occasionally resignations. The staff member needed to be aware of the personal support needs as well as the knowledge and skills needs of the committee members. It was also important to be able to see these individual needs within the overall developmental stages that groups pass through as they become cohesive working bodies.

These are the ingredients of all group processes and it is important that the group worker/facilitator was able to recognise and deal with these in the context of the work of the group. In the Family Centre, the members of the group were people who had felt a sense of incompetence and powerlessness all their lives and who now were being asked to take part in real and meaningful decision-making processes. It was an enormous challenge, but it was also a tremendous learning opportunity. The accomplishment is best expressed in the consultative processes that this committee eventually established during the final year of the first phase of the project to consult with all of the stakeholders of the project in determining the future direction and structure of the project for its second phase.

The Management Committee was the most significant of the formal groups that gave effect to the participatory goals of this project. In contrast, the Social Issues Group—while equally significant—operated as an informal semi-social Sunday afternoon discussion group. It provided an opportunity for the members of the project to share their life experiences with each other. This activity became a powerful consciousness-raising exercise where people who had assumed they were in some sense responsible for their own powerlessness began, through the telling of their stories, to realise that there was a set of circumstances larger than the personal orbit of their lives that contributed to particular groups of people being locked out of the affluence of mainstream Australia. That dependence on the vagaries of the social security system of the early 1970s or a labour market which even then was insensitive to the needs of people with family responsibilities, increased the fragility of their often-tenuous hold on affordable and secure housing. Insecure housing in turn contributed to their children's inadequate access to the opportunities offered by education, training and career paths into secure employment. This knowledge provided a powerful impetus to the social action and social change agendas of the project. It also helped to transform the member's views of themselves and their place in society.

> It is recognised that the existence of group interaction is necessary for this process of *conscientisation* to take place. The group is central to such work for conscientisation cannot be undertaken by one person on his or her own. Group support helps to carry the tensions and anxieties which a developing critical consciousness and the liberating action that must follow are found to create. The development of a critical consciousness, by which the demystification of political structures and economic relations takes place, enables a group and the individuals within it to assert their own humanity and to confront dehumanising systems. (Leonard 1975, p. 46)

A number of theorists, including Friere, contributed to the development of the project. The following quotation from Friere's work (1974, p. 16) provides some insight into the nature of the project: 'The important thing is to help men [sic] and Nations help themselves, to place them in consciously critical confrontation with their problems, to make them agents of their own recuperation'.

The Family Centre Project was a successful Australian realisation of the ideas and aspirations built into the social goals perspective. The possibilities for more work along these lines has never been more urgently needed than in the Australia of the 1990s; equally, the constraints that might prevent this from happening are strongly to the fore in the political and economic context of much community work in our time.

Review questions

1 What are the main kinds of group work identified in this chapter?
2 What are some of the strengths and the limitations of those styles of group work? Explain why you see them as such.
3 Does it really matter how we define different styles of working with groups? Explain why.
4 What is your assessment of the Brotherhood of St Laurence Family Centre Project?
5 Would such a model be applicable to any Australian context in the 1990s? If so, why? If not, why not?

Part III

Doing it

5
How groups work:
The life cycle of groups

Introduction

How do we actually work with people in groups? What are some of the hands-on issues related to working with groups? In this chapter we consider some of the practical questions involved in working with groups.

We begin with a discussion of group development and explore ideas relating to the formation of groups, stages of group development, the setting of goals and agendas, group norms and issues of conformity. We will then look at issues of power and authority. This will include thinking about questions of what has often been referred to as 'leadership' (which we call facilitation), and how this affects participation, influence and decision-making in groups. Along the way, we introduce a few strategies for group work, like how to prepare and plan for working with groups; what people mean when they talk about group diagnoses; and what kinds of strategies can be put in place for evaluating a group's activities and planning for next time.

Life cycles and stages of group development

One classic formulation for describing the life cycle of groups identifies five stages through which it is said 'all groups go'. This is the famous *Forming, Storming, Norming, Performing* and *Mourning* life cycle model of groups. We would add that stage five can often be characterised as a *Reforming* stage.

Five stages in the life cycle of groups

1 Forming
2 Storming
3 Norming
4 Performing
5 Mourning/Reforming

It is not altogether clear whether all those advocating this model of the life cycle of groups believe that this describes the stages through which all groups go, or whether it identifies what they think are the stages through which all groups *ought* to go. Watson et al., for example, claim that *all* groups develop through stages:

> Whether it is a primary or secondary classroom group, a tertiary tutorial group, a task group in an organisation or a group that meets for social reasons, a group can generally be found at one of five stages of group development. At Stage One, members are polite, they avoid conflict, they are concerned about being accepted or rejected and their orientation is towards the task. At Stage Two, group members become involved in conflict because of concerns about power, status and organisation. The 'pecking order' or 'who is good at what' needs to be sorted out. At Stage Three, there is more cohesion between members as there is more affection, open-mindedness and a willingness to share. However, the pressures to conform to the group may detract from the task at hand. At Stage Four there is a supportive group climate; however, concerns about interdependence and independence are resolved so that both can occur along with the dominant need to solve problems in a creative way. At Stage Five, which can occur after any of the first four stages, the group cohesion can break down as members are concerned about disengaging from further relationships. (Watson et al. 1980, p. 1)

Comment on generalising

We are sceptical about such generalisations. *Some* groups may go through the kinds of stages that Watson and his colleagues outline. However, this does not mean *all* groups do. There are many groups where the sequential elements of this model do not occur. Nor does it mean that all groups progress through each of the stages evenly, even when they are all present. One group may spend longer developing trust; another group may spend time establishing an operating framework (or what is called 'norming')—or they may do both things at the one time. A group may be performing in different ways for a variety of reasons—for example, they may lose a particular member or gain additional new members. This may cause participants to lose trust in each other. If this happens, the group may then need to revisit the behaviours and activities associated with the trust-forming stage. It is useful for a facilitator to be able to identify these developments in the group in order to offer appropriate support or to know when not to intervene and allow the group to find its own feet.

With time, we develop a practical wisdom about groups and their peculiarities; it is, however, important to be sensitive to the processes and dynamics that are common to the experiences of many groups. Identifying certain features of groups can help the group worker improve the capacity of people working in a group and assist members of a group to achieve both group and personal goals. All that we are stressing is the need to be careful and ensure that we do not impose our own expectations on the group. For example, we need to be sure that a group is focusing on a particular activity (say, establishing norms or trust) and not just assume this is so because of some alleged universal life cycle of group process.

We can often observe localised and particular patterns of interaction within groups. People often respond to each other in ways that are routinised or habitual, and therefore their behaviour in a group is quite often predictable (Klein 1966). For example, we know of one household where, as soon as 'mum' begins cooking dinner, her daughter complains about being hungry and immediately begins eating from the fridge. Later, when the meal is served, the daughter announces she is not hungry! Within that particular household, this is a predictable pattern of behaviour. It does not, however, mean that in every family when a meal is being prepared, another group member will begin eating. Understanding some of the features of group behaviour and appreciating how those localised behaviours can impact on group members can provide the group facilitator with useful insights for 'reading' and reflecting on group activities.

Whether you are a facilitator, a member of a committee, attending a conference or running a youth program, there are insights into the ways people interact in groups that are useful. For example, an awareness of group dynamics can assist you in becoming a more effective committee member and help you influence decision-making. You can also use these insights to help a group learn. These insights can be useful when planning a conference. You may have observed that, after the first day and a half of a conference, many participants disappear for the afternoon. This observation may indicate to you, when it comes to planning your own conference, that people have had enough after a day and a half of just sitting, listening and talking. You may then decide that building a free-time slot or an 'outside' activity into the program will improve the quality of the conference.

Moreover, if a group you are part of is experiencing a difficult period, understanding some of the dynamics of group processes can help you to provide the optimum working conditions to encourage participation.

The degree of compulsion or voluntarism involved in being a member of a particular group also seems to affect the dynamics of the groups and the extent to which questions of power or status, for example, are likely to be raised. Also, in many educational settings, emotional reactions like anger or the display of affection within a group are often kept under control in ways which the life cycle model does not always seem to recognise. Keep these qualifications in mind as we outline the elements of this model, drawing heavily on the work of Watson et al. (1980).

One thing is clear: groups change over time. Relationships between group members are different when people are just beginning to know each other, compared with when they have known each other for a considerable time (Klein 1963). It may be helpful to think of groups as consisting of different sets of relationships; it then becomes clearer that you are working with people in multiple relationships, all of whom bring diverse and unique identities, experiences and interests to the group. And all this is brought to bear on each group of which they are part.

We begin our discussion of the five stages of groups with some trepidation. The model may or may not apply to particular groups you will work with.

Stage 1—Forming: Getting to know you

What is often referred to as the 'forming' stage begins with the commonsense observation that there is an initial period in which people who may never have met each other, or worked together before, come to terms with the fact that they are in a group with others, and that they may have to spend a considerable amount of time with them. A concern of many people in the group relates to the question of whether they belong to, or can ever belong to, the group. This is a concern about their inclusion which is usually centred around hopes of belonging, acceptance and fears of rejection. Many of the insecurities we all have (to varying degrees) can emerge at this point. Am I able to speak well and clearly in front of other people? Will they like me? Do I have anything to say that will not make me look like an idiot? Can I offer anything to this group? Will I understand what is happening? Will this group give me what I want?

People can often be ambivalent about joining a group and about contributing to the group. Shyness, insecurity, anxiety, inadequacy and feeling like an outsider are some of the emotions many new members of a group experience. When most new group members feel like this, then interaction between them can be tentative and guarded. Thankfully, this awkwardness and anxiety ends when group members become more comfortable with each other and when familiarity and trust begin to develop. Regardless of the level of familiarity group members feel, when a new member joins the group (at any time) these kinds of reservations are likely to impinge on the group. Such uncertainty is a normal and common feature of human interaction that just needs time and consideration from others for it to dissipate, allowing the group to shift into a different type of relationship.

The model suggests that groups determine the nature of what will happen next. This is understood in terms of a 'need' felt by each member to contribute to the larger purpose of the group. The model speaks in terms of the *need* for people in the group to:

- relinquish the comfort of non-threatening topics and risk the possibility of revealing things about themselves;
- put aside continued discussion of the group's purposes and commit themselves to a purpose with which they may or may not agree;
- open themselves up to the risk of personal attacks which they suspect or know are just ahead in the next phase of the group.

This may describe what goes on in some groups, but it does not describe all groups.

The life cycle model is also said to involve a preoccupation with the orientation to the task. Typical behaviours at this stage are said to include people being very polite, cautious and determined to avoid conflict. Moreover, proponents of the model claim that group members are keen to raise and discuss questions like:

- What are we to do? and
- What are the goals of this group?

It is suggested that, to start the ball rolling and assist in a good group formation process, group leaders or facilitators should explicitly ask questions like:

- What are we supposed to do? and
- What are our goals?

Starting off with a new group

It is good practice when you join a new committee or new group of people to put most of your energy into observing group members and the way they go about doing things collectively. Ask questions to learn the procedures and practices of the group.

If you are the group facilitator and it is a new group, not only is it important that you get to know the other members of the group as quickly and as thoroughly as possible, but it is also important that you enable the group members to get to know you and each other positively as well.

Ice-breakers

For some groups of people, you can suggest engaging in certain activities that enable you to get to know each other. These activities are called *warm-ups* and *ice-breakers*. They may be as simple as making and drinking coffee together, making and wearing a name tag, or a form of structured activity. It may, however, be insensitive to suggest this in some groups; rather, it may be better to get on with the task that the people involved have come together to promote.

Be sensitive to your context

If you decide to use an ice-breaker, there are a few important considerations to bear in mind. For example, check whether the activity requires a lot of physical activity. If it does, it may not be suitable for some older people, or for groups with members who have a physical disability, or for heavily pregnant women. Activities that are highly competitive or that may be embarrassing for some will not 'warm' everyone up or help them get to know each other in a friendly and positive climate.

Cultural and religious differences also need to be considered. For some members, physical contact with the opposite sex—even light touching—may be taboo. This means that being required to partake in group exercises that include close physical contact is actually requiring some people to engage in culturally prohibited activities. We cannot stress enough the need to be selective and sensitive about the activities you choose for your group. Quite a few of these exercises were developed a number of years ago with young, energetic (usually) males in mind. Just because they can be found in a book does not mean they are suitable for use with all groups of people.

Group norms and conformity

During the early part of a group's existence, while establishing goals and agendas, patterns of behaviour will develop. This is what the literature refers to as 'group norms', or the rules for operating within the group. These will reflect the character of the particular group: there would be considerable variation between what was considered appropriate behaviour at the local youth group and what would be regarded as appropriate at a meeting of the local council. A group needs to be able to establish patterns that it feels comfortable with, and this pattern needs to be visible.

Groups with strong *invisible* patterns of interaction can be quite controlling of members, leading to conformity and lack of creativity. Encouragement of democratic processes allows for diversity and openness. It is probably useful at this point to revisit the four powers that we discussed in relation to the Family Centre Project in Chapter 4 and consider how they could be applied to the operation of a group so that all the members have the opportunity to grow and develop.

The four areas that contributed to a person's agency or autonomy were:

1 *Power over resources*—The skills, competencies and areas
  of knowledge we need for everyday life.
2 *Power over relationships*—The ability to work cooperatively
  with others, confident of one's own worth and contribution;
  and the security to accept the worth and contributions of
  others.
3 *Power over information*—The knowledge necessary to understand the world and one's place within it; the factors and
  relationships that locate one in a particular place within that
  world and how to manipulate those factors in order to
  achieve change.
4 *Power over decision-making*—This is the ability to syn-
  thesise the knowledge and skills that allow a person to shape
  and fashion his or her own world.

These four ideas can provide a pattern of operation for a group that
would acknowledge all members as having something valuable to
contribute and giving them the opportunity to make that contribution.

Achieving tasks and the maintenance of the group

It is important for all groups to maintain a balance between the
achievement of the group task and the maintenance of effective
working relationships between group members. Those two jobs
(achievement of task and group maintenance) need to be carefully
balanced.

The quality of the group experience can be improved if group
members have some awareness of the significance of both the task
and the maintenance aspects of group dynamics. The quality and
effectiveness of the group will be improved when all members make
a contribution to the *way* the group works, as well as towards the
tasks that the group is undertaking.

One task that needs to be undertaken to maintain the group and
achieve its goals is the seeking out by group members of the relevant
information and the views, and each other's feelings about issues
that relate to the group. This may also involve a group member in
summarising—that is, pulling together ideas and suggestions—then

restating the major points that have been discussed. Coordinating activities are also required for maintaining the group and ensuring that its goals are reached. These can include revealing relationships between different ideas, various activities and the distribution of tasks between group members.

Encouraging maximum participation is also important for maintaining the life of a group. This involves giving recognition, demonstrating acceptance and openness, and being friendly and responsive to all members. Those with a capacity to work towards creating greater harmony and consensus can play an important role in maintaining the work of groups. This may, for example, involve persuading members to constructively analyse their differences of opinion, reconciling disagreements or simply agreeing to disagree.

The ability to diagnose the 'health' of a group means being alert to difficulties or disagreements that may and do arise. Working out the reasons for difficulties and involving group members in solving them is necessary for sustaining the group. Motivating group members is another task relevant to the operation of the group. Similarly, relieving tension in the group can help maintain good working relations and produce results. This could, for example, include distracting the group with jokes or doing something silly and possibly irrelevant. After a short time, in a group that is working well, the group will usually get back on track and focus on achieving the set task/s.

The group work practitioner may take on all these jobs at various times, and each of them can improve group interaction. In taking on these roles the group facilitator can also provide a model for others to follow. Sometimes group members spontaneously perform maintenance- and task-oriented jobs like those just outlined. Ideally, the group worker will be watching for the emergence of members capable of taking on such activities, or for members with potential who could be encouraged to do so. At the end of the session, the group worker may consider it appropriate to make positive comments to the people concerned so that they and other members appreciate the value of their contributions.

It is common that a task-oriented group member emerges, doing the most to guide the discussion. Such people (there may be more than one) focus on achieving the task, and in some cases this can easily produce feelings of hostility and resentment, especially if those who are task centred become overbearing and preoccupied. This is when you may see other group members invest their energies into harmonising and resolving tension in the group.

A group needs to be kept on track in terms of its tasks; however, when maintenance of inter-group relations is ignored, the group's effectiveness is at risk. Conference planners who have built small-group discussion into their conference design often arrange for two people to take on this role in each group. In a conference setting, these two roles are referred to as the 'convenor' (who watches the group process) and the 'recorder' or 'reporter' (who is focused on seeing the group's task/s achieved).

Setting goals and developing agendas

Whatever the purpose of the group, or the stage of a group, the goals and the agendas of the group and of those within the group will be a significant factor in the life of the group. The extent to which the group can accommodate these differences will determine the success of a particular group.

A goal is an end towards which an individual or a group of individuals is working. A personal or individual goal is one that is held by an individual member of the group. A group goal is held by enough members of the group that the group can be said to be working towards its achievement. All groups have goals and every person who joins a group brings with them their personal goals. Goals can be either long or short term in nature. They guide groups by providing the purpose for which the group exists and by providing a direction for the group's efforts.

Establishing the group goal is the essential first step to establishing an effective group. Developing a common understanding of the group's purpose in coming together is necessary for establishing a common goal and a common agenda. In the process of establishing this agreement, the group members need to be able to listen to each other in a spirit of generosity and acceptance of each other's points of view and contributions. Because this is an early task in terms of the group's development, issues of power and authority tend to surface during this process. Once the goals are set, the tasks necessary to establish them become clearer and can be distributed amongst the members of the group.

At the start of this chapter, we discussed the importance of identifying the particular context of each group whilst recognising that there are generalisable patterns. It is important to restate this in relation to the consideration of group goals and agendas. If we consider some different contexts, it will become clearer that individuals bring their own understandings about what it is best to do (their personal goals and agendas), so there is a need for common understandings if the group is to work together effectively to achieve its goals. The particular group may be the management committee of a small community-based agency, a group of young people planning for a camp or a group of residents who have come together to prepare to oppose the building of a freeway in their neighbourhood. Whether you are a chairperson, a committee member, a youth worker, a concerned resident or a local councillor, you will have a particular view of what needs to be done and how it will best be achieved.

If the group is to be successful in its endeavours, then the ideas and feelings of each of the members need to be given due consideration. Group members will be more motivated to achieve group goals if they are involved in setting those goals. Maximum participation of all members is crucial in setting group goals. Democratic participation will enable members to express their personal goals, listen to and consider a range of points of view, and arrive at a common understanding. Open and frank discussion that considers a range of ideas will assist the group to become more aware of the importance of choosing appropriate goals, and will help group members to become more committed to providing resources so those goals can be achieved.

Stage 2—Storming: So who is the boss here?

The life cycle model suggests that 'storming' is the next phase in the life cycle of any group. This is said to be a more conflict-ridden time, as people let fly with questions and issues about power and who has it—or who wants it. During the 'storming' phase, people become preoccupied with who has the power or authority in the group. In this phase it is argued that some members 'resist the leader' while others make bids to take the group over. At the same time, others raise questions about how decisions will be made and who will make them. Our experience suggests that issues like this can arise at any time in the life of a group, beginning in the first minutes or in the last dying moments of a long process of group interactions.

Our sense is that there is a lot of potential for conflict and criticism within some groups while other groups seem to avoid this. Much of this conflict, when it erupts, can be expressed as concern about rules, regulations, agenda-setting and sometimes even about leadership. The textbooks usually describe this 'storming' phase by referring to certain types of behaviour, like jockeying for time, space, attention and influence. It is also suggested that, during this phase, people who are still not fully committed to the group, or who feel there is not a climate of trust or acceptance, may close off and become 'secretive'—or withdraw altogether.

Group leaders are frequently advised to ask questions and direct discussion so that these issues get an airing. It is also useful to pay some attention to clarifying possible roles for people in the group and to establish what the rules are and who makes them (Klein 1963).

The character of a group begins to take shape when patterns of communication and relationships start to develop. Group members quickly assume certain roles and responsibilities, and establish norms and ways for handling particular tasks. Power struggles can emerge between members as initial moves are made to gain greater control of the group. At such points, strong feelings of 'ownership' and a sense of belonging can become quite important to some members. This is when maintaining people's feelings and developing a positive climate in which the group can operate can be more important than being overly concerned with the tasks of the group. However, tensions like this can have their positive side. They may, for example, force members to see themselves as stakeholders in the future of the group.

Some pointers

- It is helpful to encourage all members to participate in the processes of group interactions and to keep this encouragement happening at all times throughout the life of a group.
- The group worker needs to go along with a group's choice of leader/s and work with those who seem to have support from the majority.
- Be ready for 'rebellions' and power struggles, because these can happen at any time and for any number of reasons.
- Try to conciliate power struggles or power plays, and focus the group's energies on achieving its goals.
- As leadership crises get resolved and membership becomes more cohesive, questions will be asked about the worker's role and function within the group.
- Clarify what the positive and negative aspects of increased closeness are for both the group and individuals in it.

Power, authority and leadership in the group

Power provides us with the ability to do something; however, power can take many forms. In a group setting like a youth program or a school-based committee, power is evident in the degree of influence a person has on others to get them to do as he or she wishes. In youth groups we often hear talk about peer pressure, while in a committee we may describe someone as 'being political'; these are both references to influence. Although there have been many analyses of power, authority and influence over the years, we have chosen one *typology* to help us understand power and influence:

1 *Coercive power* inspires fear and awe in the people subject to that power. It relies on threats and behaviours such as bullying and domination. A *coercive leader* relies on fear and the implicit or explicit threat of sanctions to get things done. A coercive person is often fearful of those 'higher up' and is usually a stickler for rules and regulations for him or herself as well as for others.

2 *Connection power* is based on the person's links with influential or important people (and resources) inside or outside the organisation. The leader with *powerful connections* does not have a great deal of personal confidence, hence their reliance on friends and associates.

3 *Expert power* derived from one's expertise, skill and knowledge that achieves a degree of authority and respect from group members.

4 *Information power* relies on one's possession of or access to information that is perceived by others in the group to be of value.

5 *Legitimate power* comes from the position one holds—for example, a school principal, president or director. This could be related to what Weber called 'legal rational authority', which is based on the legality of rules and on the rights of those who occupy posts of command by virtue of those rules to issue commands.

6 *Referent power* derives from one's personal traits and depends on others liking you. The closest this type of power would have come to the categories used by people like Weber would have been charismatic authority, which rests on the devotion of a group to a particular individual.

7 *Reward power* comes from one's ability to provide gains to others.

Of course, there are problems in trying to think coherently about and understand power and authority using these kinds of categories.

Coherence and order are very attractive in the midst of the complexity, tension and contradictory conditions relating to power. There certainly are limitations to developing and using such classifications. However, for the purpose of this book, such categories provide useful mechanisms for examining power and authority in groups. We often use many different forms of power (sometimes at the one time) that draw on our expertise, our position, the information we can access and the fact that we are liked. We do not claim that the power people use can be easily fitted into particular boxes, however an awareness of that complexity as described in these typologies is a useful device for investigating power relations in groups.

Power relations can be identified easily in groups like committees; similarly, they are very evident in groups of young people. For instance, coercive power that relies on the ability to generate fear, veneration and awe can be seen in schoolyard bullying. Mind you, such behaviour is certainly not restricted to young people—interpersonal bullying and stroking are also quite common amongst groups of adults. Connective power that draws on one's relationships with important people inside or outside the organisation is often apparent in the students who traditionally are labelled 'teacher's pets'. Expert power, which is based on a claim to expertise and skills, is what gives sporting heroes, musicians and fashion experts their power and status. Examples of legitimate power can be seen in the standing and authority attributed to a team captain or school prefect. All group members, regardless of their age, ethnicity or gender, have varying degrees of ability to influence.

It is helpful to be conscious of the nature of power relations within a group for three reasons:

1 You will be in a better position to increase your own agency and therefore have some capacity to help shape events and issues that concern you.
2 An appreciation of power alliances and sources of power will provide a better understanding of why people act as they do.
3 With such an awareness, you may be less likely to be intimidated by such *powerful* people.

However, the question remains of how you can use such insights to increase the operations of the group in positive ways. A few pointers to achieve this include:

• valuing yourself and what you know;

- being prepared to assist others in the group and to share what you know;
- asking questions, speaking out about matters that you consider important, and being open to new ideas or different ways of seeing things that will improve the quality of the group's procedures;
- exchanging new ideas with others, asking for advice and being prepared to modify your own position;
- keeping an open mind;
- listening to as many views as possible before making up your own mind and being aware of your own prejudices.

Someone who has a negative approach and who is continuously critical of activities and others will also usually have little power. This is not to say that dissent and critique are bad things for a group. Dissent should not be confused with conflict. The encouragement of dissent and the ability to maintain a climate in which dissent is welcome and seen as a valuable part of the group is necessary if the group is to be able to cope with change and operate in democratic ways. Tolerance of conflicting views and a questioning of the right of one individual or group to have the monopoly on what is best or right are evident if there is an appreciation of dissent by members in the group.

There are many ways in which a group (or members of it) can maintain its existing power relations. One way is to suppress dissent, which can be achieved in many ways. It can, for example, be done by simply excluding those who disagree, by isolating them or demonising them, or by employing tactics in the group that result in dissent being interpreted as betrayal or heresy.

Constant and continuous criticism without producing new ideas and or a commitment to action for the development of positive future options can be a destructive force in a group. Group members who have a generally positive attitude to others and the world around them, who are receptive to new ideas and who see dissent or critique as a means of developing better options are more likely to be listened to and therefore have more influence within the group. One strategy for making a group function more effectively is to accompany critique with viable alternatives.

Leadership or facilitation?

There is a prevailing view that leaders are born, not made. One of the founders of Western philosophy, Aristotle, claimed that from the hour of our birth some of us are marked for subjugation and others for command. This approach to leadership suggests that it cannot be learned and implies that some people have inherent characteristics that enable them to be leaders. Alternatively, it has been suggested that different leadership positions require different kinds of leaders—that being a good facilitator is something that can be studied and learnt. We agree more with this position.

With the aim of effective group work in mind, what are some of the important features of good leadership? Or rather, what are some of the features of being a good facilitator? Changing the term here from 'leader' to 'facilitator' says something important about the way we think about the question of styles of 'group leadership'. Leadership does imply a political position *vis-a-vis* other people, which may not work in all the varieties of groups in which group work is being done, or which may not help to achieve the aims and objectives of a lot of groups.

Many of the traits found in good facilitators can also be found in followers. These traits include self-assurance, an interest in others, a willingness to learn from others, generosity and a healthy self-esteem. The best rule for deciding what are the necessary qualities required of a facilitator for a particular group is to look at the goal/s of the group and then select a person or people who displays the necessary skills and motivation to help the group achieve its goals. Alternatively you may decide that your group does not want or need a facilitator.

If we look at history, or even the contemporary world around us, it is clear that leaders have had (and continue to have) an immense influence. We need only think of the military and charismatic leadership of male leaders like Napoleon, Hitler or Stalin, or female leaders like Joan of Arc, or think of the political and intellectual leadership provided by Queen Elizabeth I, the medical and health care leadership of Florence Nightingale, and the political leadership of Golda Meier, Indira Ghandi and Margaret Thatcher to realise just what a difference leaders can make. As Giddens explains, 'A leader capable of pursuing dynamic policies and able to generate a mass following or someone who can radically alter pre-existing modes of thought can overturn a previously established order of things.' (Giddens 1991, p. 658)

Like the literature on power, that on facilitation is vast and identifies many different types of facilitators. For simplicity's sake, we refer here to three broad styles of facilitator: the *authoritarian, democratic* and *laissez-faire*. Of course, it is not always possible to identify a facilitator who fits neatly into one or other of these types. You will probably be able to think of facilitators you know who sometimes could be seen as authoritarian while on other occasions they are democratic. In short, a typology is just a shorthand mental device to render the real mess and chaos of the reality we live in briefly accessible and manageable. So long as we don't confuse typologies with reality, we should not get too confused or lost. Talking about facilitators in these simplified ways does allow us to at least open up some issues for debate about the ways in which leadership styles can affect group processes.

Despite our experiences as leaders, whether we be the prime minister of the nation or the Pope, there is always room for further development of our leadership capacity by thinking about what makes for good leadership and by working more cooperatively. Take, for example, committee work and the role of chairing—there is no dispute that learning how to be a chairperson is also about learning to be a leader—or more often, these days, a facilitator.

The authoritarian facilitator

Authoritarian facilitators tend to believe they know what is best for other group members and set about directing the group. This may take the form of paternalism and guardianship: it is based on the assumption held by the facilitator (and often by others in the group) that the facilitator knows what is good for the group and individuals within it.

Typically, such facilitators set the group's goals, policies and strategies, allocating tasks and expecting people to obey directives. Such facilitators also tend to assume that the group will go along with the instructions and may be surprised when disagreements, suspicion and reluctance to carry out tasks develop. This authoritarian approach to facilitation is useful and appropriate in certain situations, such as in emergency circumstances. Directing emergency workers in a natural disaster or crisis situation where there are many urgent tasks to be undertaken may well require authoritarian styles of facilitation.

Democratic facilitator styles

Our ideas about democracy owe much to the eighteenth century and draw on the notion of visible and legitimate authority. They also draw on the idea that democratic citizens observe the conditions of their group and its context and discuss them with each other. The result is a shared enterprise and the development of trust in leaders. Whether leaders deserve such trust depends on how well they merit that trust (Sennett 1993). Democratic leaders are a part of this tradition and, as such, seek the maximum amount of participation and involvement from the group in decision-making, attempting to negotiate and share responsibility.

Laissez-faire or permissive leadership

Laissez-faire leaders neither consult nor direct. Their style is similar to a free-market ideology applied to a group setting. Group members are left to go it alone, to do as they please, and nobody is expected to take responsibility. This type of leadership can be effective in some situations where there is equally shared expertise and a con-scientious commitment to an agreed task. The *laissez-faire* or market idea banishes the authority of the leader and in its place depends on a system of exchange.

Stage 3—Norming: Getting on together

In the life cycle model of groups, 'norming' is said to be the stage at which a real spirit of 'togetherness' begins to emerge in the group, with a lot more evidence of cohesion as members start to think more about the group as a whole and contribute to its cohesion. Issues of trust get to be central to the success or failure of the group. People in the group at this stage are said to become preoccupied with the degree of trust and affection between themselves and other members. This is the stage during which people joke more, relax more and show a greater willingness to share information and to open up to other people in the group. There is usually a big improvement in the quality of team spirit and teamwork.

It certainly seems reasonable to suggest that, as time goes by, and in groups where people seem to be getting on with each other, most group members will tend to feel secure and make greater efforts to change the things that make people uncomfortable or slow down the group's activity. A sense of cohesiveness or group identity can develop. This is a often good time for getting on with the job by giving priority to achieving tasks. Without task-directed activities at this point, it is easy for some groups to become preoccupied with 'navel gazing'—that is, being too concerned with feelings and relationships instead of getting on with the job of reaching their goals.

Some pointers

- Try to write down the ideas and values that people agree upon and those that they reject.
- Encourage group members to remember already agreed group goals and set common objectives.
- Clarify positive and negative aspects of increased closeness.
- Acknowledge growing independence as an interdependent group.
- Detect and point out those aspects which may be forming obstacles and obscuring the common ground between members.

Stage 4—Performing: Getting on with the job

Performing is the stage during which group members begin to realise that the group's life must come to an end. The group is at its most 'groupy', with people expressing concern about interdependence and independence, and members all showing evidence of a high level of commitment to the group. There is evidence of a concern to get on with the purpose of the group and to engage in creative problem-solving of issues confronting the group. Where there is evidence of conflict between different people in the group, there is now also evidence of a willingness to agree to disagree.

With time, group members may tend to become more open with each other, although sometimes, given the personalities of certain people, this may never happen. Leadership and responsibility may become more evenly shared as a result. The group may also become better organised and more efficient. These conditions can provide a good working climate for a group, whether it be a committee, a work team, a school class, or a youth group.

Some pointers

- Give recognition to the people who are working hard to get the job done.

- Celebrate success and milestones along the path to achieving group goals.
- Help to develop new objectives for the group.

The literature describes a fifth stage in the process of group development. This stage applies to groups which have been established for a particular purpose; once the purpose has been achieved, the group disbands. The time leading up to the end of a group can be quite turbulent or quite sad. The literature refers to it as the 'mourning' or 'reforming' stage.

Stage 5—Mourning/reforming

Mourning is the stage in which people recognise that the group is ending and/or changing. Members may need support to successfully disengage from the group. It is important that participants are able to see this as a natural part of change and growth. Now is a good time to evaluate what was learned from the group, and what can be taken away from the group. People need to assert their individuality and separateness from the group. Participants may start to get angry with the leader, while displaying increased warmth to the other group members. There is often a marked breakdown in group skills and far more lethargy; with increased efforts being made to work well as a group, the focus on the original task can be lost. It is often more appropriate to deal with process issues around the end of the group than to keep on addressing content issues. There is a sense of dislocation and lack of focus. In this sense, some people—and even some group leaders—*maunder;* this means that members and leaders engage in 'idle incoherent or rambling talk' which interferes with, or in bad cases can abort, the group process.

Avoid *maundering* in this stage by:

- planning to address the sense of loss and grief as the 'parting of the group' approaches;
- assisting members to undertake new tasks and directions; and
- placing attention and emphasis on reflection and evaluation of the group's achievements.

Group goals have been achieved, members have learnt new skills, knowledge or behaviours and are ready to move on to something else. This is particularly common with groups of young people. They enter into a club or a group activity at 15 or 16, but their interests and abilities are very different two or three years later; the activity of the group is no longer meaningful, while the friendships continue to matter. Sometimes even these may lose their significance as young people leave school and move on to different destinations. In these situations, it is important to recognise these symptoms and perhaps revisit the processes that were helpful in the 'getting on together stage', as they help people come to terms with changes in themselves and evolving relationships.

The tools of group work

The tools of the group facilitator are the same as the tools for being an effective member of a group. They largely consist of consciously developed interpersonal skills, good observation techniques and a sound working knowledge of the elements of what we have discussed in this chapter. Interpersonal skills are the skills we all use every time we interact with each other: being able to express your ideas clearly and unambiguously, and being able to listen, hear and respond to other people's ideas. The democratic process is dependent on this two-way responsibility for understanding; when it is not taking place, difficulties arise.

Observation techniques coupled with an understanding of group process result in being able to diagnose problems and propose remedies. Here is a list of questions that will help you understand why a group may be experiencing difficulty.

Checklist for interpersonal communication skills

1 How are members expressing themselves? Are some aggressive, non-participative? Are they saying what they mean?
2 How well do members listen to each other?
3 How do members respond to each other? Are they critical of others' ideas, concerned for self? Do they ignore each other?

How democratic is the communication pattern?

4 Is everybody contributing? Do people address each other, is all

the communication directed at one person? Do some people get listened to more than others?

Is the group moving towards achieving its purpose?

5 What is the content? Is it relevant? Is it task-oriented or maintenance-oriented?

Is the leadership style appropriate to the task?

6 What style of leadership is being displayed—democratic, authoritarian, *laissez-faire*?

7 How is the group responding to the leadership style? Are members eagerly participating? Is there a high or low commitment to the activities and ideas? Is there a lack of enthusiasm, resisting of ideas, holding back on contributing?

What is the climate of the group?

8 Are people pleased to be there? Do they start out by greeting each other and showing interest in each other before getting down to the particular business of that meeting?

9 Is there a sense of cohesion and cooperation?

How clearly are the goals understood and accepted?

10 Are the goals still appropriate? Are they still clearly understood or do group members need a reminder? Are group members still committed to each other and to their purpose?

The group worker needs to be constantly monitoring the group process, checking the climate and the purposefulness of the group and interjecting the appropriate prompt when it is required (energiser, explainer, tension reliever, reminding of focus, etc.).

Evaluation of the experience and planning for next time

Just as a good committee member has read the report of the last meeting and is familiar with the agenda for the current meeting, so the group worker has preparatory tasks for each group session. The responsible and professional practitioner will spend some time reflecting and evaluating on what has happened—this is part of planning for the next step. It is important that group workers structure into their work a process for analysing, for examining alternatives and possible outcomes, before leading a session and for working out what it is hoped that the group will achieve as clearly as possible before each session, as well as consciously evaluating how it went afterwards. The checklist of questions provided above is a good starting point.

Evaluation

At its simplest, evaluation involves asking:

- What happened?
- How well did it work?
- What could be changed?
- Where do we go from here?

At this level, evaluation is a tool for the facilitator. Evaluation is also a crucial instrument for any worker. It is the means by which we ensure that we are providing the best possible service and it is an important factor in our own learning. Because it involves asking the relevant questions of ourselves, as well as the members of the group, reflecting on the answers and seeking new and improved ways of doing things, evaluation is the tool that will maintain and develop effective and worthwhile learning experiences for the group as well as for the group worker.

Conclusion

Often, one cannot simply just decide to be a facilitator. The opportunities for and success of facilitation do not depend just on the qualities of the individual facilitator, but also on whether the social conditions and quality of relationships within a group are favourable for effective facilitation to develop. In political terms, this is certainly true for leadership. Prime Minister Margaret Thatcher, for example, was able to take political power and leadership in England in the late 1970s partly due to the fiscal, economic and social conditions that plagued England at the time. Had those conditions not existed, it is unlikely that Mrs Thatcher and her 'revolutionary' libertarian-market interventions would have had the impact that they did on the Western world.

Facilitation is based on a capacity to manage social relationships effectively. Like any relationship, it cannot work well unless there is reciprocity. In other words, having a facilitator requires having people who will support that facilitator. A facilitator needs to maintain the confidence and faith of the group in his or her capacity to act effectively as a facilitator.

We have discussed the issue of 'leadership' and facilitation in the context of working with groups in ways that assist people to work together to achieve more than they would as individuals, as well as to experience the group context as a place for personal learning and development. In the next chapter, we discuss the value of group work more specifically in the education context.

Review questions

1 Why is it important to recognise different stages of development in groups?
2 Think of a group with which you are associated. How has this group developed over time?
3 Which style of leadership/facilitation do you prefer? Why?

6

Working with groups: Structured experiences and experiential learning

Introduction

Traditionally, the teaching of people who want to work with groups has relied on an experiential approach. Experiential learning is about learning through doing, and relies on using 'structured exercises' that have been developed to assist this process. Experiential learning has a much wider application to teaching people who want to work with groups. In this chapter, we will look at group work in a learning context. Groups are central to experiential leaning, whether action learning, team learning, adventure-based learning or collaborative learning (Boud et al. 1993). Experiential learning engages the learner in what is being learnt and provides the opportunity to use experience as a 'teacher'.

Learning together in groups provides people with a different learning experience from that found in the traditional classroom or lecture theatre (Weil & McGill 1989). It also requires different kinds of skills. This means that the 'teacher' stops being an authority figure and possessor of all the knowledge, and moves into the role of facilitator described in the previous chapter. Experience becomes the teacher and the 'teacher' role is to support and resource this to happen. Participants are encouraged to do and to reflect and then, with their peers and the facilitator, make meaning out of what has been experienced (McGill & Beatty 1992). We are not saying that this kind of learning is new—quite the opposite, in fact. Learning from our experience is as old as humanity itself. Human beings have always learned from their experiences and then theorised about them. ('Theory' from the ancient Greek word *theoria* is best translated as 'reflection on practice'.)

Good experiential learning in groups depends on a high level of cooperation amongst the members of a group. In many organisations today, there is a strong commitment to collective decision-making. As Brown puts it:

> . . . people are to be involved in making decisions and encouraged to take responsibility for their own actions. This value is based on the belief that people should be respected for their views and abilities. Besides the increasing evidence that cooperation yields more successful results in solving problems than does competition . . . the participation of persons in joint decision-making can build self-esteem and bonding within the group. (Brown 1991, p. 85)

In a more general sense, cooperation is the crucial ingredient of purposeful and effective groups.

> Group work makes cooperative rather than competitive learning possible, for the emphasis is on group tasks and group achievements. (Gale 1974, p. 6)

As we will suggest later, collaborative group work with an effective facilitator can best be defined as a form of transformational group work, because the active learning that results enables participants to be involved in changing their own understandings of themselves and their world (Boud et al. 1993).

What is learning?

There is a lot of nonsense talked about what learning is—or is not. There is, for example, a long tradition in experimental psychology which equates learning with being able to memorise things like long strings of numbers, or nonsense words. We think there's a lot more to learning than being able to memorise things. And even though we are academics, we also think learning is pretty straightforward.

Learning

Learning is what happens when you can do or think or be something or someone you couldn't do or think or be before.

Don't get us wrong. Learning can certainly involve memorising formulas, lines of poetry, remembering the colours and designs of a painting or remembering how to make a chocolate cake. But that is a relatively shallow way of approaching learning. Learning is a far richer and more interesting process than just memorising things. Learning is also about making new connections and achieving new insights. It can involve a new insight into your 'self'. It may involve making judgments about the beauty of a certain dance step, or working out how to advise a violinist about improving her bowing technique. It may be about acquiring some knowledge about our collective history or getting some insight into the meanings of a word. It may be about figuring out a shortcut on a new word processing program on your computer. In an important sense, the real stuff of learning can't be forgotten since it goes into making us the person we are constantly becoming.

Inevitably, learning is a creative process, and there is always something of a minor miracle about it. Once one of our children, then an eighteen-month-old little boy called Jamie, was just learning to talk. One summer's day around lunchtime we were out on a walk down a dusty country lane. Jamie stopped to pick up a daisy. He looked at it. He held it up in the air and then pronounced, 'Like the sun'. That's learning.

Learning in groups

Many of the best parts of working in groups come about from the possibilities for learning from being in that group. And much of the best kinds of learning that goes on in groups comes about in experiential ways (Boud et al. 1993).

- Experiential learning in groups refers to the learning that proceeds from the experience of group members.
- Time is provided for members of the group to make sense of these experiences by observation, reflection and evaluation.
- In experiential learning, observations are absorbed into and shape or reshape theories, concepts and ideas (Tyson 1989, p. 155). There are also a number of other models of experiential learning that have been developed by theorists like Argyris & Schon (1978) and McGill & Beatty (1992).

Experiential learning

The 'learning-by-doing' approach has been an important part of educating young children, older students and anyone entering vocational fields for a long time. For hundreds of years, what we now call the 'apprenticeship system' provided a basic and simple method by which young people learned a range of skills, as well as developing a capacity to make wise and practical judgments and to develop insights. This was the way plumbers, doctors, carpenters, lawyers, farmers, midwives, teachers, architects, coopers and smiths learned their trade. Then, some time in the nineteenth century, people began to think it would be better if people went into colleges and universities to learn these trades on a proper professional or vocational basis.

The 'learning-by-doing' approach has recently been 'rediscovered' by professional educators, trainers and other human service workers, as an effective approach to learning in a wide range of settings (Boud et al. 1985). Some of us think that there should never have been any need to 'rediscover' this, and that the rediscovery is testimony more to the problem of collective amnesia or of professionals needing to reinvent the wheel to demonstrate that they are up to date.

This 'rediscovery' and revival of interest in experiential learning has led to the development of a new body of literature and to a 'new' method of education called *experiential education.* (Boud et al. 1993; Evans 1994). Experiential learning is very powerful as a way of learning because it offers a body of direct personal experience upon which we can then reflect and learn from. For people working with groups, this has meant recognising that an excellent way to develop good insights into the ways groups work and the value of working with groups is to use an experiential approach to learning and/or teaching these insights and skills.

Four reasons for using experiential learning

1 *Experiential learning is about learning cooperative working styles. Working together is a vehicle for bringing together groups of people, and creating more democratic work cultures.* We need to encourage a return to democratic and collaborative work cultures, especially if people are to recover control over their lives (Emery & Emery 1974). Ours is a time when democratic values and practices are under threat from a very successful 'counter-

revolution' by modern managers and economic fundamentalists who insist on competitive, individualist and market-based values. This is justified on the grounds of introducing 'flexibility' and 'choice', but it actually creates arenas in which the strong get stronger and the weak get lost.

2 *In many areas of contemporary professional education (like nursing, teaching or interpersonal communications), people are rediscovering the value of practice-based and workplace education.* Many modern professional courses use a lot of learning through field education, or through student placements in hospitals, schools and businesses. The student teacher, cook, nurse, accountant, doctor or programmer learns a lot by doing. They learn many things this way that could never be 'taught' by the best or most experienced classroom based teacher. They learn by engaging in supervised work within the hospital wards, offices, social work agencies or classrooms.

3 *Experiential learning values and recognises and draws on previous experience.* It may suit teachers of a more traditional kind to think that valuable learning can only take place through their teaching. But good teachers have always known that the experiences and insights you bring with you into a classroom are important and need to be linked with new learning processes. Prior learning is increasingly being counted and taken into account, through credits and exemptions being granted when people enrol in particular university courses.

4 *Experiential learning, for instance, may include learning or developing particular personal skills like the ability to listen well and to actually hear what people are saying, or to use body language in ways that are consistent with what you are actually saying.* This may sound like a simple thing to do, but watching carefully as people talk to each other will show that many people are not good listeners.

Structured exercises

Modern approaches to learning how to work with groups have been solidly based on experiential learning approaches, typically built around the use of *structured experiences*. The idea of providing 'experiential' opportunities to encourage learning through reflection on action has meant increasing use of *structured exercises*.

Group workers use structured experiences that are designed to engage us emotionally, intellectually and/or creatively (Evans 1994).

Sometimes they require physical and play-like activity. Good structured experiences require thinking and feeling in a reflective way on the part of group members. They generally work best when they draw on cooperative behaviours and attitudes. Even where the structured experience looks like a game, we should not automatically assume that the 'aim of the game' is to win. The idea is *not* to have winners and losers. Structured experiences that use games are designed to encourage learning about how people individually, and groups collectively, deal with the processes and outcomes of the activity. Structured activities that are designed thoughtfully, and that are facilitated effectively, can provide a positive experience for all the members of a group. Structured exercises can make contributions to general education as well as helping to develop group work-based knowledge, skills and theories.

However, this is not to deny that there are some structured exercises and experiences whose value is dubious and whose continued use reflects an inability on the part of group leaders and group work teachers to reflect on their own experience. Some group work teachers stay locked into techniques they learned a long time ago, and refuse to keep on thinking or revising their approach.

Experiential learning in groups using structured exercises

As we saw in Chapter 2, modern 'scientific' experiential learning and action research effectively began with the work of Kurt Lewin and his colleagues in the 1940s, when they began to research the dynamics of group activity and developed special techniques for human relations training. These were subsequently developed by Carl Rogers and his associates at the National Training Laboratories. Drawing on the work of Kurt Lewin, researcher David Kolb developed the idea of the 'experiential learning cycle'.

Experiential group work creates a situation of continuous learning through the life of the group. Experiential learning involves making an effort to become aware of the often automatic modes of thinking and behaviour we use collectively and personally in particular settings (Evans 1994). Structured exercises are used widely by many different occupational and voluntary groups, particularly in areas such as education/training, recreation and in the voluntary sector as part of the training of volunteers. Structured experiences involve learning about groups and interpersonal behaviours 'by doing', and then by reflecting on the doing.

Structured exercises

Structured exercises are often:

> . . . an organised game-like activity designed to produce group processes that can be easily understood by participants. [They are] easily understood because the processes will have just been manifested in the participants' experiences throughout the game. (Watson et al. 1980, p. 1)

Structured exercises are commonly used throughout the whole human service sector. They can be found in universities, schools, youth work agencies, women's refuges, juvenile justice and rehabilitation centres, attendant care and so on.

It is useful to look at the following examples of group work settings and purposes where structured exercises are appropriate.

Leadership issues

- Where leadership issues are concerned, structured exercises are important to help in deciding what the facilitator and/or group members believe the group needs to know in terms of their knowledge or skills. We give you an example of how this might be done in an example in the box below. Try to think about how you might set about achieving some of the other objectives using structured experiences.

Example

How do we establish whether group members want a leader and, if they do, what kind of leader they want and who in the group has the ability and desire to be a leader? This can be done, for example, through a structured activity. Working through these issues can be done in the following way:

- Begin by asking a volunteer in the group to make a note of the discussions and report a summary of the discussion back to the group at the conclusion of the activity.

- Give each group member a sheet which contains the sentence, 'My specific fears of being designated the leader of a group are . . .' and ask that they write down their response.
- These sheets are then collected and the contents discussed amongst the group members. After each statement is read out, members suggest ways of reducing that concern.
- The group reconvenes and a summary of the concerns and solutions and unsolved issues are re-examined with the facilitator.

- There are lots of other possible uses to be made of structured exercises.

Ice-breaking

- Sometimes when a new group is formed or when a new person is introduced to an old group, there may be some value in setting up a little experience to help 'break the ice'. So how do we introduce people new to a group or to each other with an exercise designed to work as an 'ice-breaker'?

  It can be quite useful for people new to a group to be introduced to the group in ways which help them to present themselves as they would wish. People often get introduced to a group in ad hoc and informal ways, and while this may work well, sometimes it may not work at all. A good group process gives people who need to work with each other the chance to get to know each other in friendly and non-threatening ways.

Group processes

- Observing group processes in action, and getting some insight into how interpersonal behaviours work and don't work in group settings, is vital. Teachers of group work frequently use structured exercises to simulate group processes so that the logic and dynamics of the group can be more easily and clearly seen—this enables group processes and dynamics to be better understood because structured experiences, if designed and done well, can reveal the underlying logics and dynamics of a group.
- Structured exercises can serve to review particular problems and

issues, like dealing with someone who is upset about another person in the group. Many groups of people deal badly, or not at all, with interpersonal problems and difficulties that crop up from time to time in groups. People form stereotypes and expectations of other people which are not always felt to be right or appropriate. Or people's working and relating styles can clash. This is especially the case in male–female relationships, where all sorts of behaviours and gestures can be interpreted on both sides of the gender divide as 'problems'. Again, effective group processes can help to clarify what is going on and lead to a recognition that some behaviours and gestures may need to be modified.

Innovation

- Exploring new relationships between ideas and practice in a work setting can be done through structured exercises. Many modern organisations like to talk about how progressive and interested they are in developing new ideas and practices, while they actually keep on doing the same old stuff. Universities are a classic instance of this—indeed, they are possibly the worst example. University teachers use teaching techniques like 'the lecture', which are hundreds of years old. They defend the use of this quite dubious technique to the death, while waffling on about how committed they are to sustaining a culture of learning. The sad truth is that most 'organisations' are conservative and their personnel don't like the sediment of old practices to be disturbed. Yet, in the 1990s, there is a real case to be made for promoting change in thinking and action. Good group processes can create a safe haven for new ideas and proposals to be floated.

Strategic planning

- Structured exercises provide opportunities to think about future events or to plan for new programs or activities in an organisation. Increasingly, many work organisations are scheduling a regular time each year to look ahead, build 'team spirit', plan budgets, propose new programs and evaluate the past year. (Many of these activities are called 'retreats' in silent homage to the legacy of the monastery whence this practice originated.) Again, a well-planned retreat which uses appropriate and sensitively designed group exercises can really help an organisation to do its job well. Equally, bad retreats can blow the life out of a team and even bring on a bad case of demoralisation. (Many bad retreats begin when the organisation decides to hire an outside consultant at vast expense who turns out to be incompetent.)

What kinds of exercises can you imagine or design that might help to address the kinds of issues just identified?

- leadership issues and styles of facilitation;
- ice breaking;
- innovation;
- strategic planning;
- observing group dynamics.

Examples of structured exercises

These examples have been chosen because of their suitability to illustrate the principles that we identified as being important for the development of structured exercises. They can, of course, be used in a range of situations and will probably work better if they are modified to suit the particular circumstances and characteristics of a specific group.

1 *Each activity should have at least one clearly articulated learning outcome.* This means that the group leader or facilitator must be able to specify precisely what they want group members to learn and why, and how the structured· activity will actually help to achieve the learning goal.

Example

The desired learning outcome is to increase participants' powers of observation of communication patterns in group discussions. An exercise that is designed to achieve this aim might look like this:

One member of a group is asked to 'map' the group by drawing a circle and listing the names of each member on the location at which they are sitting. That member then moves to sit outside the group and begins to draw an arrow each time a group member speaks, connecting it to the person addressed by that speaker. (When a person speaks generally to the group, just draw the arrow into the centre of the circle.) This goes on for about five minutes. At the end of the five minutes, questions can be posed like this:

- Who has spoken the most?
- To whom were most comments aimed?
- Who is generally silent?
- What efforts were made to bring quieter people into the discussion?
- What shifts, if any, took place in the interactions over time?

---

2 *Activities should thoughtfully and sensitively reflect the interests, skills, abilities and experiences of the participants in the group you are working with.* This means that group members should have a strong sense that the structured exercises reflect and complement their own experiences and their identities.

Example

You are working for the first time with a mixed-gender group of people with severe physical disabilities. It is also their first time as a group. Their disabilities include confinement to large motorised wheelchairs and limited control of physical movements. Only two of the people in the group can speak and be understood easily. The rest use a variety of keyboard-driven ticker tape and voice machines.

Communication in this group is very slow. In addition, assembling and ending the group can take half an hour at the beginning and end of the group session and the group has to be able to meet in a venue with good ramp access for wheelchairs. Any exercise has to be designed to accommodate (among other things) the very slow process involved in group communication.

Design an 'ice-breaking' exercise that takes these difficulties into account.

3 *The capacity for learning should be enhanced by encouraging participants to take a slight risk, experiment and/or try out some solutions or ways of acting that are different from what they might normally do, in ways that are safe.* By its very nature, learning is about acquiring some new insight or skill. Equally, we should also recognise that good learning takes place when people are not feeling anxious, upset or scared. Good group processes should involve a high degree of sensitivity to any signs of distress or anxiety on the part of group members, and be able to terminate an experience or modify it quickly if a member shows any sign of distress.

Example

The group is a feminist group comprising only young women aged 18–25 years. The exercise is centred around problem-solving particular issues in each member's family relationships. Group members would need to feel comfortable with each other and a high level of trust and mutual support would be required for this kind of exercise to work well.

The design might include an element of role-playing in which one member at a time chooses a real issue and plays herself. She also recruits a few of the other members in the group, and gives them a role like 'mum', 'dad', 'brother', 'sister', etc. The central 'character' then gives them a partial 'script' around an issue like how arguments get started in the family or how the family addresses a particular problem like the drinking of one of the parents. They have ten minutes in which to develop the role-play and the group as a whole then comments on the situation, the logic of the action and so on.

This is clearly going to involve some risk-taking, and the group facilitator should be prepared to help the people playing the roles if they begin to re-create certain anxieties or bad feelings. This should be done in ways which try to give each person a sense that it is OK to have the problem and the feelings that go with it, thus not closing off the feelings or involving censorship or excessive nurturance, which can lead to a discounting of the problem. A clear indication of the limits and the capacity to alter or end the role-play as needed would be clearly communicated to the group at the start of the exercise.

4 *The creative abilities of participants are engaged.* This means that, in any effective structured experience, the game or experience should call in some authentic way on people's imaginative, playful and creative capacities.

Example

You are working with a group of young teenagers aged between 12 and 14 years of age. They are going to engage soon in a one-week school experience placement at a nearby 'retirement village', so you are doing some preliminary exercises with them. You say:

'It is said that old people's homes and villages are sad places because all the old people are there because they are waiting to die and are surrounded by people just like themselves. The fact that there are no young people or children there makes that problem worse. Put yourself in the place of those old people. Pretend your group is made up of residents of an older people's village. How do members of the group feel about living in the village? In your role as an older person and as a group of older people, identify some of the positive things about living there. Discuss this among yourselves for fifteen minutes.

---

5 Opportunities are created whereby participants are encouraged to get on with each other and to initiate and engage in cooperative activities. By and large, this means that good learning in groups draws on the interactions of group members and uses the shared sense of working together. When this happens, it can create a very powerful feeling, almost amounting to a 'high'.

Example

There is a very famous structured exercise called 'Prisoners' Dilemma'. (It can be found in any number of manuals, like Watson et al. 1980.) This game sets up a situation of conflict to see how well a group of people can work through a situation logically designed to promote competition and conflict. The point of the game is that cooler reflection will soon suggest that cooperation is more effective for everyone than competition.

The elegant simplicity of this exercise has never been bettered, and the issues it raises—such as how enlightened self-interest can lead to an ethos of cooperation—are profoundly important.

6 It is important that the structured activities can draw on a wide range of learning styles and preferences. Creating good learning opportunities recognises that people learn in different ways and that people operate with different cognitive styles. Howard Gardiner calls this recognising 'multiple intelligences'. Some people like lots of visual or written material to react to, while others prefer listening and others would rather be doing or playing because they are highly tactile.

Example

You are teaching an adult group of learners in a TAFE program or a Neighbourhood House. The participants are working on a Tertiary Bridging Program, which they hope will prepare them for entry to a university course the following year. You want to help each member of the group to discover how they learn best, so you have prepared four different kinds of input, each running for between ten and fifteen minutes.

Note: each presentation covers a different topic, although each relates to the others They include:

1 a standard chalk and talk mini-lecture with minimal overheads;
2 a short video tape which is heavily reliant on illustrations, with minimal voice-over;
3 a short audio tape with plenty of voice-over and music;
4 a short activities project which involves a fair bit of touching and working with hands.

These presentations are to be run over a day with an hour at the end of the day for evaluation by each member of which style of presentation they found most insightful and illuminating.

Problems with structured experiences

Having identified the positive value of structured exercises in working with groups, let's turn to the other side of the coin. There are many books and commercial manuals on the market which offer hundreds of examples of structured activities. With this choice in front of us, it is not always easy to be discerning in the activities we choose. There is clearly a body of useful practice wisdom wrapped up in the evolution of many of the classic structured exercises. But times, conditions, attitudes and understandings change and develop over time. Many of these older exercises do not reflect the changes that have occurred in terms of:

* the way work is done;
* gender roles;
* multiculturalism;
* young people's access to information;
* the use of language;
* hanging values.

Ours is a culture increasingly devoted to the idea of the 'quick fix', a clear sign of the dominance of professionals whose very life and income depends in part on persuading us that 'they' have a 'quick fix' up their sleeves. We go to doctors for a pill to fix what often only discipline, dieting and hard exercising will 'cure', or we imagine that a few hours for family therapy will fix a problem that has taken years to develop. And, more generally, with all sorts of new technologies like e-mail and the fax machine, we expect things to be done faster and faster; the fast food industry depends in part on this mindset. It is not surprising that some group workers encourage us to reach for 'off-the-shelf', ready-made structured exercises.

Despite the array of choices available to us, the best structured activities may often be the ones that you design yourself. It is critically important that we understand some of the ways in which structured experiences can produce useful formative and beneficial learning experiences, while also appreciating some of the theories that underpin their application, and at the same time appreciating their limitations.

Structured experiences *can* provide positive and enjoyable opportunities to learn. A very good set of learning exercises was devised by Tricia Szirom at the YWCA in the 1980s for use in all-female groups for women who wanted to explore how to be effective *as women* in often threatening and insensitive male-dominated organisations. This is a form of group work with a very explicit gender politics that informs a highly appropriate and carefully designed set of structured experiences.

Unfortunately, structured experiences can also cause considerable discomfort and pain to individual members of a group. One of us recalls vividly a group led by a particularly insensitive and dim-witted group leader who decided to use the famous structured experience called 'Lifeboat'. This 'game' involves people having to make decisions and justify their answers about who cannot get into a crowded lifeboat with limited space. The group leader ignored the fact that several of the group members were Vietnamese people who had come to Australia' as 'boat people'. Each of them had recent and very raw memories of travelling long distances in an open boat, facing danger, hunger, pirates and the constant threat of violent death on a daily basis. These people were very upset when this group leader pushed on, insensitive to the obvious distress the exercise was producing.

Likewise, not every group needs or wants to play 'ice-breaking' games if members already know each other. Groups with predominantly political purposes that are made up of mature-age, experienced and committed people may well think—probably rightly—that most of the structured experiences many group workers have at their fingertips are a waste of time. In this setting, it may be better to aim, for example, at a straightforward exercise of introductions, in which people identify themselves or their organisation, or outline their reason for attending the group.

Towards a thoughtful approach to the development and use of structured exercises

In this book, we want to encourage a thoughtful and careful approach to the development and use of structured exercises. The whole thrust of our book has been to insist on the need to avoid over-generalising about the commonality of groups and to both recognise and to respond to the rich, interesting and specific textures of each group.

There is value in recognising the highly specific nature of particular groups, and therefore there is value in designing some specific structured exercises for *that* group. This means:

* If you design the structured activity with some insight into or knowledge of the group, the activity is more likely to be better and more useful than any 'off-the-rack' kind.

- If done well, the structured activity you tailor yourself can match the character and competencies of the specific group.
- It is also more likely that it will meet the particular needs of group members.
- Developing a structured experience is very similar to the type of work that teachers and those involved in curriculum design do all the time. When you develop structured experiences you are in effect designing a curriculum.

What does 'curriculum' mean?

A broad understanding of 'curriculum' defines it as: 'the sum total of aims and objectives, ideas, activities and every process that provides the basis for the learning experiences of a group of people to take place'. Based on this, 'curriculum' is more than just the plans for teaching or group activities and more than, say, a set of readings or a package of structured activities: it includes these things, but also includes the social relations that are set up, the use of physical space and time, the way the session is conducted and the style of facilitation, as well as any assessment or evaluation processes.

We now summarise the things you need to take into account in designing some of this group work curriculum.

Four basic questions about structured experiences

Four basic questions

Whether you are planning to use other people's structured experiences or to develop your own, you need to ask some basic questions before you do anything else:

1　Who is in the group, and how do the different identities of group members (e.g. gender, ethnicity, disabilities, ages of members, etc.) affect the group process?
2　What are the aims and objectives of the group?
3　What are your own abilities as a facilitator?
4　In what ways do you plan to reflect on, monitor and evaluate the progress of the group's activities?

---

1 *Who is in the group and how do the different identities of group members affect the group process?* Asking who the group is, and who each member in the group is, forces you to consider the group's identity from a number of viewpoints. For example, you may ask who they are both collectively and individually. In other words, who do *they* think they are? Is there agreement—or at least some consensus—in their view of themselves? What is their status in the host organisation? You may find, for example, that the group has a distinctly and even radically different view of who they are and what their objectives are compared with the institution in which they exist. How do you deal with this?

How do those different perceptions of the group's collective identity impact on the workings of the group, the resources allocated, the objectives set and the likelihood of achieving them? This may also mean thinking about things such as the ethnic composition and the gender breakdown of the group. It may mean considering the ages and social and biographical experiences of the people in the group. Finding out about the group members' collective background and gaining some information on the personal histories of people in the group can also be useful.

2 *What are the aims and objectives of the individual people in this group and the group collectively?* Clarifying the aims and objectives of the group is important, especially when the people in the group are not clear about this. You need to establish the aims and objectives you wish to achieve *before* you can design and develop activities that are directed towards achieving those ends. You might also need to establish what (if any) internal and external constraints on the group and people within it exist. How do you expect those constraints to impact on the group dynamics and the group's ability to realise the declared objectives?

3 *If you are to be the leader or facilitator, what are your own abilities as a facilitator?* How do you relate personally and professionally to the group and to the people within it? What kinds of insights do you have about your own strengths and weaknesses? It is a matter of continuing surprise how often group work facilitators lack a degree of insight into their own capabilities and their personal strengths and weaknesses.

4 *In what ways do you plan to reflect on, monitor and evaluate the progress of the group's activities?* How do you see the role of structured experiences working as part of a developmental and learning culture that you want to see evolving within the group? Do you, for example, intend to involve the group in those

activities, and if so, for what purposes and in what ways? What kinds of monitoring do you propose to carry out? Will it be via a questionnaire or some other instrument? Or will verbal feedback do?

This is probably the right place to comment briefly on the issue of diversity in groups.

Designing gender-sensitive structured activities

Developing a sensitive structured experience means being aware of and receptive to the basic kinds of 'identity markers'. These include people's gender, their sexual preferences, their ethnicity, their culture, their religion and their political commitments, together with any other 'markers' that people feel strongly about. Here we focus on the question of gender.

In developing a structured experience, the first question is how we develop a gender-sensitive activity. This is not a simple question, since it may raise a lot of related issues. Do we work with a single-gender group because the bulk of the women are feminist separatists who feel uncomfortable about working with men? Can we get agreement on a 'gender inclusive' principle? Do we mainstream the group or do we create two groups, one for each gender?

In developing gender-inclusive activities, attention needs to be paid to a number of principles and objectives. These include challenging the masculinist knowledge base that still dominates many group work teaching programs in the 1990s. It also requires that gender be made a central and inclusive component of human service curricula in ways that are alive to the diversity of experiences and self-identities of women and men. Recognition of the principle of difference is then less likely to be overlooked in the effort to achieve greater equity.

Gender-sensitive structured experiences also draw attention to the implications of power imbalances. They involve asking questions such as: What are the power and gender implications when leadership positions in education, government and community agencies are dominated by men? What are the possible ramifications of power imbalances in relation to sexual relations and unwanted sexual interaction occurring between colleagues and between workers and managers?

In developing gender-sensitive activities, the facilitator needs:

- to have a secure grasp of the gendered nature of contemporary work sites and practices, especially in the human services area;
- to be well informed about current work-site industrial laws and practices, and equal opportunity and affirmative action legislation and how these things can impact on organisational practices; and
- have insight and skill in establishing working relations that respect gender issues and sensitivities.

The following points may help to identify the role of gender when you are deciding whether to adapt already existing structured experiences or to develop new structured experiences. They include:

- giving consideration to gender issues that are involved in the formation of the self and in the construction of particular social roles. This is necessary if you are planning to intervene effectively and skilfully with your group;
- ensuring that you have knowledge and skills which will enable you to deal both sensitively and ethically with gender issues that arise in your own work site and in relation to your group;
- being able to deal in constructive ways with the gendered divisions of labour and gender-based expectations within the group and the agencies in which members work.

Some more general principles for the development of structured exercises

1 *Each activity should have at least one learning outcome that is clearly spelled out.* These days, teachers, trainers and group workers are increasingly accepting that quality learning is about them being able to specify a learning objective, in ways that are quite detailed. Similarly, it is good practice for any group facilitator who wants to be effective to be able to specify quite clearly what he or she wants the members of the group to be able to do or to think that was not possible before.

2 *Activities should thoughtfully and sensitively reflect the interests,*

skills, abilities and experiences of the participants in the group you are working with.

3 *The capacity for learning should be enhanced by encouraging participants to take a slight risk, experiment and/or try out some solutions or ways of acting that are different from what they might normally do, and do so in ways that are safe.*

4 *The creative abilities of participants are engaged.*

5 *Opportunities are created whereby participants are encouraged to get on with each other and to initiate and engage in cooperative activities.*

6 *It is important that the structured activities can draw on a wide range of learning styles and preferences.*

A final point:

7 *Participants usually gain more from the structured experience if they reflect on and evaluate the learning which took place.*

All of this brings us to a final word on the role of the 'facilitator' or 'group leader', as some people still refer to this role. We believe that the attitude, values and skill level of the facilitator are fundamental to the nature and quality of the participants' experience in these exercises. We pick up on this issue in the next chapter.

Conclusion

Collaborative processes for problem-solving activities in groups are very useful. Such activities produce a greater reserve of material or ideas to draw on. They also provide members of a group with an opportunity to appreciate the value and benefits of collective decision-making, and can help to accelerate the opportunities for good learning. This type of decision-making is especially crucial for all organisations attempting to initiate change—it is imperative for both large and small organisations. This includes a regard for the sense of ownership experienced by participants. When members feel they have helped determine decisions that will affect them, they are more likely to be cooperative at the implementation stage because not only are they informed about the changes, but they have helped make the changes. Collective decision-making means participants are aware of some of the constraints operating at the time those decisions are made—such as budgetary, legal or policy constraints. Such knowledge may prevent resentment because preferred alternatives were not taken up.

The benefits of cooperative group work include its capacity to help develop people's self-esteem and their sociability. It allows members to have fun just for the sake of it, or to enjoy themselves while gaining and refining knowledge and skills. There are also moral justifications offered for the use of cooperative and experiential group work, especially when it involves collective decision-making. To be responsible, it is important to be a party to determinations that influence our own actions and shape who we are. To be moral, it is necessary to consider and take responsibility for our own actions.

As mentioned, the type of collaborative and transformational group work we are talking about can take many forms. When the intention is to engage people in a learning experience that will enable them to integrate the known with the new in order to develop new personal learning, it can also be said to develop the agency of the individual participant. This is our particular interest in this chapter on experiential learning and the place of structured exercises.

Review questions

1 What are the different kinds of learning that are talked about in this chapter? What do you think of our 'definition' of learning?
2 Think of a recent learning situation that suited you. What was it that helped you learn? How would you define or describe the kind of learning that happened?
3 Develop, run through and then evaluate a structured exercise which helps you address one of the following issues:

   • leadership issues and styles of facilitation;
   • ice breaking;
   • innovation;
   • strategic planning;
   • observing group dynamics.

7
Working with groups and the role of the facilitator

Introduction

Throughout this book, we have stressed the need to be sensitive to difference. We have argued against assuming that there is a single set of 'scientific' truths that we can draw on when we are working with people in groups. In this chapter, we look at the role of the facilitator—or what is sometimes still referred to as the 'leader'.

It is the responsibility of all professionals to exercise not just due care in carrying out their work but to ensure that their skills and understanding are appropriate to the work they are doing and to the people with whom they are working. The values and attitudes of the facilitator in a group are at least as important as his or her expertise and level of 'skill'.

To explore the role of the facilitator, we have developed a case study that illustrates why this is important. This case study also provides material that will help to develop greater understanding and insight on the part both of facilitators and those who are participants in group work. This material can be used as a structured exercise if desired.

The role of the facilitator

Without being overly prescriptive, it nonetheless seems sensible to make sure that some of the following aspects of the facilitator's role are clearly understood. (We have used the example of a group about to use a structured experience, but with modifications this protocol could be used for a number of purposes.)

The major responsibility of any facilitator is to ensure that the structured exercises and the general processes work as smoothly as possible, and in ways that are consistent with the learning goals of the group.

Prior to the session, the following preparation should take place:

- You should know what your role in any group work process is to be.
- You should have any materials ready and prepared.
- The physical environment should be properly set up—chairs in the right places, appropriate heating and lighting, etc.
- You should make sure that adequate time has been allowed for all activities.
- You should explain the rules and directions for carrying out the structured experience as simply and as clearly as possible.
- Choose observers if these are required. It is often very useful to have one observer looking on as a structured exercise is carried out.

During the structured exercises:

- Keep the exercise moving along.
- Explaining the rules or processes.
- Answer any questions clearly, simply and so everyone can hear what is being said.
- If the group hits a sticky spot, or is not entirely clear what ought to be done next, the facilitator should suggest that the group take time out for some discussion, in an effort to achieve some consensus before proceeding.

The best way to maximise learning and reflection is to have the members of the group do the hard work—the thinking, the talking and the analysis. This implies that, immediately following the structured exercise, there must be enough time left for reflection, analysis and discussion to take place. Failure to plan properly can lead to frustration and to lost opportunities to learn from reflection in this part of the session.

After the structured experience:

- Let the discussion and reflection flow and encourage members to engage in this process.

- Pose some large and open-ended questions like:
  - How did you experience that exercise?
  - Was that exercise close to what happens in the 'real' world?
  - How could it be made to fit better with the 'real' world?

Only make these kinds of insightful contributions if they haven't already been made and the session is running out of time. By and large, it works better if the important insights can come from the members of the group. This implies that generally it is *not* for you as the facilitator to say what has been learned, what matters or what is really important.

The main role for the facilitator through a structured experience is to watch and observe the process in action and the ways in which each member of the group deals with the experience. It is *not* appropriate for the facilitator to pass judgments about members of the group, or how they are handling the group/exercise either verbally or by some use of body language that implies some negative judgment. Facilitators must aim to be really disciplined and not engage in editorial comment.

In the next part of this chapter, we will show how certain questions, reference points and principles can be applied to an actual group.

Styles of facilitation: Introduction to the Blue Gums scenario

It is very problematic to talk and think about groups of people as if they are all more or less the same or all have the same features. For this reason, we have developed an exercise centred around different facilitation styles. We look at two different styles of leader and imagine a situation where each style of facilitation deals with the same group, called here the Blue Gums group. We want to use this profile to demonstrate how to apply basic curriculum design principles when developing structured activities that are effective for a particular group. At the same time, we will illustrate how different perceptions of leadership/facilitation influence our perceptions of those who are to be facilitated or led. This is particularly important if the objective of group work is to develop the *agency* of group members.

We propose to develop one potential scenario and then to imagine the different experiences that the scenario would provide for the participants depending on the style of facilitation that has been employed. We have two styles of facilitation:

1 authoritarian facilitator style; and
2 democratic facilitator style.

The context

The group, which is made up of students in a welfare degree course, is on a residential 'camp' in early March. It is high summer and the days are very hot. The camp is a compulsory component of the group work subject (which is also a compulsory core unit in their degree). They are staying for two nights and three days in a holiday camp on the coast outside Sydney.

The stated aims of the group for the next few days include:

• Group members are to get to know each other. This is considered important by some staff within the university department for developing what is referred to as 'group unity', or cohesion. The idea is that such cohesion will enhance the learning experience throughout the year.

• Facilitators want to teach a number of group work skills and to impart some group work knowledge.

• Participants should gain experience in the organisation and general running of a residential group work experience.

A profile of the Blue Gums group

The group comprises eighteen young people, most of whom are in their early twenties, although five are in their thirties and forties.

They are mostly Australian-born, with the exception of three people. One young woman was born in Bosnia and another is a Malay male from Malaysia—both of whom are practising Muslims. The final foreign-born student is a Timorese-born young woman.

The group is mixed in terms of gender, with ten women and eight men. All are group work students who are undertaking the second year of a welfare degree.

Scenario 1—The authoritarian facilitator

In this first scenario, the group work facilitator is someone who works in a quite traditional authoritarian and highly interventionist way. He is a senior academic with a pompous manner and is in his late forties. His body language is typically perceived by some, especially women, as slightly menacing. He usually avoids direct eye contact with people to whom he is speaking. He is well known for his lack of reciprocal regard for anyone except people more senior in rank than he. He talks a lot in his groups about empowerment, but generally insists on telling his groups what they should have learned. He has been known to 'tell off' students in his groups for inappropriate behaviours or responses.

At the start of the camp, the facilitator hands out a list of the structured experiences that will be covered during the three-day program. The program for this experience is one that the facilitator has conducted before. He expects that students will enjoy the exercises and will learn aspects of group dynamics through their experience of the structured exercises. He also expects that participation in these exercises will result in the development of group cohesion through the participants 'getting to know each other' through the residential experience.

Pause for reflection

How will this facilitator deal with the particular group and what will be his effect on the group?

In this scenario, a number of assumptions are clearly operating, given that this facilitator is in charge. It is worth taking the time out to question a few of them. The most obvious assumption is that there is a lot of educational value—that is, 'opportunities for learning'—in using structured activities. A second assumption is that the living together experience develops cohesion and cooperation. If you were a facilitator it is helpful to consider whether you would agree with these assumptions.

Ideally, it is good if all group members participate in deciding what value there is in having structured activities, and such a discussion can easily be part of a goal-setting dialogue. Involving group members in decision-making processes that determine what they, as a group, are going to do and what they are going to gain from the activities is more likely to produce positive results than excluding them from such decision-making.

If group members think about and resolve whether or not the group work they are to be involved in is of value to them, they will be clear about what is happening, the direction that group activities are going to take and the reasons why such learning experiences are happening. Learning will be more focused if students are given the opportunity to reflect on their learning needs and plan in the light of the expected experience. Giving group members some choice and the chance to shape their experiences is likely to establish a stake by group members in the experience.

The opportunity to provide members with the chance to have a say about processes and outcomes is not always available. In settings like the one described above, the agenda had already been set along with the activities. In other similar environments, like schools and youth training centres, the objectives and nature of the group work are usually undertaken without reference to the group members. This can be experienced as a loss of agency, as the members feel that they are (once again) at the receiving end of someone else's 'good idea'.

The following questions can inform the development of curriculum.

Who is the group?

Asking who the group is from the viewpoint of the university department in which members are students may produce an answer like: 'They are undergraduate students undertaking a particular vocationally oriented degree'.

From the two teachers' perspectives, there are likely to be two quite separate views. (There may be a shared view about who the group is, or there may be some points of agreement and some disagreement, but this is unlikely.) The students themselves may have a variety of opinions about who they are both collectively and individually.

What often happens is that this question is simply not asked. If the question is not asked, then particular assumptions are made about who 'they' and 'we' are. Often, there can be quite a disparity between the identity of the group as perceived by different members. It may, for example, be assumed by both teachers/facilitators that they both (of course) know who the group is because it is obvious. Furthermore, both facilitators may assume that the other identifies the group in the same way he or she has. However, it may soon become apparent that each facilitator has different conceptions and aspirations. This can cause problems later on, especially when it comes to developing the structured experiences.

Asking who the group is also forces you to consider the group's identity—hopefully from a number of viewpoints. This information is valuable for designing the learning experiences. And, as already mentioned, it also reveals possible disagreement about who 'they' and 'we' are. In the Blue Gums group, this question would have revealed that the two facilitators had quite different ideas about who the group was.

The senior facilitator saw it as a group of relatively passive recipients of information who were privileged both to be university students and in the particular course and should accept his facilitation as a rare measure of good luck. Moreover, he felt that the students did not have very much to contribute to the learning experience. He 'had' the knowledge and the authority to determine what they needed to learn and how it ought to be learnt, and he felt they owed him respect. Finally, this group leader (who had given up a break at his beach house to be at the residential group and who wasn't in the slightest bit resentful) believed before he had even met the group that many of them did not want to be there and that they felt resentful about it being compulsory.

The other facilitator (the democratic facilitator) saw the group differently. She believed that quite a few in the group were excited about the residential group and had high expectations about what they were going to learn. She saw group members as having experiences and knowledge that could be useful in determining outcomes and processes, and she wanted to encourage maximum participation in setting the goals.

The students all had quite varying ideas about who they were collectively. This ranged from some who accepted the idea that they were there just to receive particular sets of knowledge and skills to others who considered that they already had years of practical group-related experiences and wanted to have that acknowledged.

Pause for reflection

- What is the status of the authority or power behind each of the different perceptions of the group's identity?
- Can you predict the nature of the experience that these people will have over the three-day program?

In one sense, the status of the Blue Gums group had already been determined by the senior academic staff in charge of the curriculum. The senior facilitator had already assumed authority. The structured experience and syllabus had already been determined by him before the start of the residential without consultation with the other facilitator or with students, and he was not keen to open it up to further discussion. Equally it is also plain that there were people in this situation who had radically different views about who the group was, and what its objectives were.

How would you deal with this scenario?

This is a big question, the answer to which may lie in simply trying to establish productive and positive dialogue between the parties concerned (between the two facilitators initially, and then with the students as a group).

Likely outcomes

Do the different perceptions of the group's identity impact on the workings of the group? The answer is usually 'yes'!

If, for example, a number of students have considerable experience and that is not acknowledged, it is likely (amongst other things) that not only will there be resentment, but also considerable boredom because they will be taught knowledge and skills they are already very familiar with. Depending on the confidence levels of the group members, they may challenge the authority of the facilitator. How would you predict that an authoritarian leader would respond to conflict?

Ignoring the cultural makeup of the group, or its gender composition, can lead to quite disastrous and even destructive outcomes. It can result in the application of structured activities that are inappropriate for this particular group of individuals, with the potential for creating very unpleasant, hostile, harmful consequences that are injurious to both the individuals and the group collectively.

For example, being sensitive to the ethnic background and cultural histories of group members—who in this case include two practising Muslims—would preclude the use of activities such as 'Rocking the Cradle' which require close physical contact to develop trust. People from a Muslim tradition would find this offensive and embarrassing in a mixed-gender group.

Clarifying the aims and objectives of the group

For those who see the role of the student as one of passive learner and that of the facilitators as one of authority and expertise with the duty to impart knowledge, then the expectation is likely to be that those with the knowledge should tell 'us' what 'we' need to know. For those who want to be involved in determining the nature and shape of their own learning experiences, their exclusion from this process may cause disillusionment and resentment.

With this group, the objectives have been predetermined by the senior facilitator. Many of the others in the group are left wondering what those objectives are and how they are related to the activities in which they are engaging.

The constraints on the group and people within it again differed in line with the varying ideas about who the group were and their reasons for being there. The primary constraint from the second facilitator's perspective was that the process of establishing who the group was, what its objectives were and how it could achieve those goals excluded most group members, including her.

Scenario 2—the democratic facilitator

In this second scenario, there are also two group work facilitators. The senior academic has a doctorate in Women's Studies and has turned to group work as part of a strong feminist commitment. She is shortish, with a low but pleasant voice and maintains easy and regular eye contact. She almost always wears clothes that are colourful. She smiles a lot. She enjoys excellent rapport with most of her students, although a few of the men in her groups are often wary for some time. She favours a quite open style of facilitation, which— as she defines it—means beginning by working with the group to develop aims and objectives as well as determining what kinds of processes the group as a whole will engage in. Her objectives for this group are that the participants develop the necessary skills and confidence to work developmentally with groups. She believes this learning is likely to be most effective through experiential activities. The facilitator also clarifies with the participants whether some of students-as-team-members have different agendas to others within their group—including her own. This involves clarifying exactly what the group members see as an effective team, what its objectives are and what processes would be required for achieving those goals.

This preliminary work provides a shared understanding from which to proceed and a clear direction for the group.

Pause for reflection

This very fundamental and preparatory work often seems so basic that, all too frequently, groups assume a common understanding of what a good team is and of the objectives.

How will this style of facilitator deal with this particular group and what will her effect on the group be? Again, there are assumptions operating here. The first assumption is that this group is able to contribute to its own learning and will be able to assist in developing a learning experience. She also assumes that the personal feelings—that is, the self-confidence levels—of the participants are an important consideration. On this occasion, the facilitator does not presume to know who or what the group is until she has checked it out with them. The 'who are you?' question is put to the group as a whole (including group members and facilitators). As a facilitator, it is helpful to consider whether you agree with these assumptions.

Who is the group?

A dialogue was established which took up the first two hours of the group work process. At the end of this, there was some consensus:

- The group was made up of members of an undergraduate group work class who had a particular interest in team work, and in analysing how to plan and manage Human Services.
- Some members of the group also had other ways of identifying themselves and other group members now became aware of those differences (for example, gender, age, level of experience) in the group and how these may have an impact on the group's functioning.

The facilitator then asked, 'We all know what a team is and we all know what working together well means—or do we?'

Beginning with a common or shared view of the specific tasks required to reach the agreed upon plan of action means that you are less likely to get halfway into a program only to discover that some members of the group have very different ideas about what a team is, how it works effectively, and what the team's objectives are and how they ought to be achieved. Some team members, for example, may have clear and strong views about the appropriate roles of men compared with those of women. For example, one or more members may believe that the men ought to be in charge of the important things. Other members may have strong views about the importance of all members being equally responsible for 'important' matters. Moreover, you may find team members who believe that an effective team requires a strong autocratic leader, while others in the group assume collective and democratic decision-making are necessary.

Although it is important for the group to be clear what their specific views of a team are, there are a few features of groups that can help define them as a team. Groups of people—whether you call them teams, families, work groups, clubs or departments—are not abstract units that exist outside their particular context and distant from their histories and other peculiarities. Groups are alive, always shifting, tension-ridden units about which we can neither offer simplicities nor glib generalisations. The character, needs and objectives of groups always differ from one another. Some groups share certain features in common with others and this cannot be denied, but we do need to be careful of the long-standing assumption that groups can exist as entities waiting to have some general definition dropped on them. This is why we think that the group itself—with the help of the facilitator—should define itself (as a team, centre, club or family) and work towards establishing its own objectives and the processes by which it achieves them. (This is also why we encourage facilitators to develop their own structured experiences.)

The same applies to the process of establishing some common aims and objectives. Given the chance, the Blue Gums group is able, collectively, to agree that it is interested in learning about group work, with some of those who already have some prior experience being acknowledged as having some expertise. The group is therefore readily able to establish that, among its aims, is that of gaining some insights about how to manage a Human Services group of workers.

Following on from this, the students and facilitators also agree that the facilitators should get together and design a set of learning and assessment tasks that are to be undertaken by the students as they work with each other in small groups. Similarly, it is agreed that the students will be graded on both the content of their individual work and their ability to work together.

How would you deal with this scenario?

How can a facilitator-cum-teacher judge the ability of the group to work together? How can the diversity of experience in this group become an advantage rather than a difficulty?

Likely outcomes

The Blue Gums group in this scenario has already clarified what is meant by working together effectively, so everyone is quite clear about what criteria are to be used to assess how well group members are working together.

One further agreed-upon objective of the first two sessions of the residential was that the students should get the chance to view themselves as a working team. (In Scenario 1, this objective was pre-empted.) Before the program got underway, a consensus had been established about what constituted a team.

The group maintained that, in order to work together effectively, it would be valuable to be introduced to some of the strategies for doing this. The resources of the group were assessed and it was established that the facilitator should lead the introduction, calling on the experiences of some of those in the group who had worked in teams before coming to the residential.

How to use these scenarios

First choice

As the reader, you can assume that you have come as one of the two facilitators. You are relatively new to the department, you have not worked with the other facilitator before and you do not know the group you are working with.

First, develop a plan of action to ensure that you can make a contribution to the program. Second, identify what it is you hope to learn as a result of the program. And third, discuss how you will evaluate the success of your first two objectives.

Second choice

Use this material as the basis for a set of group work structured exercises. That is, you may wish to use these two different scenarios once each as the basis for a structured experience. This could be done by:

- creating a group that is a replica of one of the Blue Gums group;
- setting up a role-play for each of the styles of the facilitators.

Notes for use of this material as a structured experience

The objective of this structured experience is to demonstrate how different styles of leadership can help produce significant differences in terms of outcomes.

Things to do

- Ask for eight to ten volunteers to be members of one group, and ask for another eight to ten volunteers to be members of the other group.
- You will need another four people (two per group) to be facilitators; they can choose which of the two styles of facilitator (i.e. authoritarian or democratic) they want to be. Give each of these people a briefing sheet based on the material from the scenarios appropriate to their role.
- Make sure they have time to familiarise themselves with the tasks and roles outlined on the briefing sheets.
- Ask for one person to be the observer for each of the two groups and to record their observations.
- Ask the leaders to return to their groups and commence the activity.

Observers

Your task is to observe your group. Pay particular attention to what the facilitator (or leader) does at the meeting. Watch how members respond and consider the ways in which decisions are reached. Record also the tone or feeling of the meeting. You are a non-participant observer. You will be required to report your observations to the whole group at the end of the activity, commenting in particular on the differences that you observe between the two styles of leadership and how you saw those different styles impact on the outcomes of the meetings.

At the end of the activity—whole class discussion

Ask observers to report, and allow the groups to respond to the descriptions of their activities. After the reporting, ask the class to focus on the differences and the effectiveness of the two meetings in terms of getting a job done, sense of satisfaction of the participants and the way they would describe the leadership styles of the facilitators. Make it clear to the group that the facilitators were working to a script. As the teacher, it is important to introduce the concepts of leadership style and the application of different styles to different settings (i.e. autocratic may be appropriate for directing work at the scene of a disaster such as a train derailment, but what would be more appropriate for a group of students working on a group task?) Where might a democratic approach be appropriate?

Remember to leave enough time for reflection, feedback and analysis when you are designing the session.

What are your own abilities as a facilitator?

How do you attempt to establish a dialogue that opens up the possibility of a more inclusive decision-making process without causing offence to those who believe otherwise?

Do you routinely reflect on, monitor and evaluate the progress of the groups with whom you work? In the Blue Gums case, evaluation discussions at the end of each day provided the basis for feedback and the opportunity for feedback to shape the learning experiences planned for the next day.

Review questions

1 Think about the actions of the first facilitator. What can you say about his attitudes and values in relation to group work?
2 How are these different from those of the second facilitator?

8

Working with groups in community work and social movements

Exercise: Breaking balloons

The procedure is as follows: each participant is to blow up a balloon and tie it to his or her ankle with a string. Then, when the coordinator gives the signal, the participants try to break one another's balloons by stepping on them. The person whose balloon is broken is 'out', and must sit and watch from the sidelines. The last person to have an unbroken balloon is the winner. The participants can then discuss their feelings of aggression, defence, defeat and victory . . . (Johnson & Johnson 1987, p. 299)

Introduction

Somewhere around the world at this moment, people in groups are blowing up, then standing on each other's balloons before discussing their feelings about it. At the same time, people in other groups are blowing up other people, as part of some process of 'ethnic cleansing'. Some people are playing at history and others are making it.

In this chapter, we address the challenge of using group work to make history. As we will show, group work is a vital part both of *community work* and of *social movements* (Touraine 1981; 1987). Group work can be very useful when it sets out to assist people to gain a new community service or to achieve freedom from oppression or injustice (Briscoe & Thomas 1977). In fact, group work has a major role to play in promoting social change. Understanding how

165

to work with groups can help promote effective community development and assist social movements to achieve their objectives.

Community work and *social movements* are the product of men and women addressing questions like 'why can't we have a school that meets our needs?' or 'why do we have to put up with non-existent public transport?' Working in groups is a means of bringing people together to achieve shared objectives and offers the basis for organising people to work together effectively.

The context

It is blindingly apparent that Australia is currently a society undergoing unprecedented change. All too often, however, change is something that many of us experience as something that other people do to us. At the end of the twentieth century, Australians are caught up in waves of social, economic, political and cultural change. Barry Jones has suggested that what we are going through now is a Post-Industrial Revolution (Jones 1982). This is partly to do with the ways in which we now work. We are changing *what* we produce and *how* we produce. Two-thirds of Australian workers no longer make things (like cars or shoes), but instead produce information, symbols and services. The coming of the Internet heralds a move away from large-scale hierarchical organisations and allows much more work to be done from home offices, as well as the increasingly non-face-to-face education and communication patterns. In the personal and public worlds, we are also slowly changing the old sexual division of labour between men and women. Until the 1970s, men went 'out' each day to work, to make money and decisions. Most married women stayed at home in the 'private sphere' to carry out the household work and to bear and rear children. Now half of all married women work for income. We are also changing the basic patterns of family life and sexual relationships (with new styles of family life including gay marriages). No longer do two-thirds of young Australians leave school at the age of 16; more young people are combining part-time work and education or training into their mid-twenties while, at the other end of the life cycle, the retirement age is falling as younger men and women leave the full-time work force.

Radical changes are also marking the relationship between Australian governments and the economy as governments sell off utilities like electricity and water, contract out their work and services, and generally try to reduce the scale of government interventions. The major political parties seem increasingly distanced from the main concerns of electors and appear to have 'lost the plot'. Some of these changes are also producing a more unequal society (Wills 1995). Australia seems to be confronting a future of permanent unemployment. In late 1996, we still had an official unemployment rate of nearly 9 per cent of the labour force, although considerable 'hidden' unemployment means that the real rate of joblessness is much higher. Young people are especially vulnerable to unemployment, with a youth unemployment rate of around 25 per cent. Australians are also looking at permanent underemployment.

The list of changes we are experiencing could go on and on. Two questions seem inescapable as we near the end of the twentieth century:

---

1 How do we make sense of, or 'explain' these changes?
2 What can or should we do about any of these changes?

How we ask these and related questions can help shape the kinds of answers we come up with.

How we develop the 'right' kind of questions and the answers does matter for a book on group work. Remember that we are arguing that group work has a key role to play in promoting social change. Yet who is the 'who' that is caught up in social change and what is 'social change' anyway?

'Individuals' and social change

Many Australians would perhaps begin by saying that social change affects all of us as 'individuals'. This in turn can quickly lead on to asking what the 'individual' can do about technology, mass unemployment—or nuclear war, world poverty or global warming, for that matter. It is not surprising, when we put the question like this, that many of us quickly decide it is all too hard and that we may just as well give up any attempt to think, let alone do anything about such issues.

To pose the question in this way is to set up the small 'insignificant' person that you or I is often said to be against the might of billions of dollars' worth of equipment and the combined authority and weight of the major corporations, elites and governments of the world. It is an unequal battle from the start.

We need to begin in some other way. We might, for instance, raise questions about how we understand connections between what have traditionally been defined as 'personal' or 'individual' issues on the one hand, and as 'structural' issues on the other. For example, how do we think about or address widespread social problems that may be experienced or felt as a personal problem—for example, the fact that I am unemployed and feel miserable because my family is sometimes hungry.

People who work in the welfare industry often turn this difference (between 'individual' and 'structural' issues) into a hard and fast distinction and see solutions to the problem as involving a choice between different professional forms of intervention. This might involve choosing between doing 'therapeutic' or one-to-one interventions like casework (often done by social workers) and taking more 'structural' approaches like 'community work' or 'policy development', or forms of social action characteristic of social movements, on the other. These binary splits (like casework *versus* community work) are frequently assumed to define something real. We doubt, however, that this is ever really the case. What many people call 'individual' experience is often much more a 'social' experience.

In fact, what is frequently defined as an 'individual' experience is rarely that. Troubling experiences that feel very 'personal'—like being depressed—are shared by hundreds, even thousands, of people—and for the same reasons. Worrying about where the next meal is to come from, or how 'that' bill can be paid, can be felt as a deeply personal worry, but again these things have been experienced by many of us. Similarly, many of us feel personally angry about a government decision, but again we are not alone in this.

The point is that many of the things we do on a daily basis and experience as purely a personal activity are profoundly *social* activities. Simple things like talking to someone else, giving a seminar to an audience or being part of a protest rally are all forms of social action. This is not to say that each of these social actions has the same scale of social effect. If we use the metaphor of different sizes of pebbles being dropped into a pond producing larger or smaller ripples, some of our social actions are small pebbles affecting only a few people, while larger stones affect more people. What determines the difference in effects is firstly the different ways we think about how we are going to achieve social action and social change. And this is determined by such factors as the number of people we want to involve in the process of change. Moreover, the difference in the scale of the effect we achieve may also be shaped by the nature of *what* we want to change. Changing a piece of bad legislation may affect large numbers of people, while changing the position of a traffic light may affect only a small number.

Many years ago, C. Wright Mills (1970, pp. 11–12) talked about what he called 'the sociological imagination':

> [It is] a quality of mind that will help people to use information and to develop reason in order to achieve lucid summations of what is going on in the world and of what may be happening within themselves.
>
> The sociological imagination enables its possessor to understand the larger historical scene in terms of its meaning for the inner life and the external career of a variety of individuals . . . The sociological imagination enables us to grasp history and biography and the relationships between the two within society.

Many of those sociologists who have admired Mills' statement over the past 25 years have nonetheless failed to do what he was calling for.

Good work with groups should help all of the participants in a group to grasp both history and biography within their own specific social setting. Group work can play a key role in promoting social change. Groups and group work have all sorts of advantages over individuals pursuing change. Any kind of change is a bit like trying to drive a car at high speed while redesigning the engine. It is definitely something you should never do alone. It can even be fatal! Get in a few friends to help make the changes and share the driving. People working in groups have been central to many of the major social movements of the past half-century. Group work and social change make a powerful partnership. But not any old group can produce social change.

And this brings us to the other question: what is social change? This question leads to another problem diametrically opposite to that of individualising everything. We can also end up 'sociologising' everything so that the problem gets defined as something only 'society' can handle; the result is the same—paralysis and inaction.

What is social change?

Social change ought to be a simple issue, since it seems to deal with all forms of change affecting people and their relationships. However, if it is applied to all the changes with which we are familiar, such as people getting born, married, divorced, dying, changing jobs or even changing our 'favourite' TV shows, it might run the risk of becoming over-used to the point where it means nothing.

Social change is a hard concept to think about, partly because sociologists and the way they think about 'society' and the 'individual' have got in the way and confused some of the issues. Too many sociologists have talked about 'social change' as something involving whole systems called 'society'. Some sociologists then distinguished between change which was 'good' for society and change which was 'bad'. Worse, the idea of social change defined it as a process that affected the whole 'structure of society'. Hence people talked about Social Change in the form of Big Processes like the 'Industrial Revolution' and 'Class Struggle'—some even collapsed all of the past two or three centuries into categories like 'Modernisation'. These sociologists could then go about asking questions like: How much is 'social change' the product of 'Technology'?—or 'Science'?—or 'Class Conflict'?

This way of posing the questions and developing the answers had one unfortunate effect: sociologists treated ordinary people as if they were just puppets dangling at the end of strings pulled by impersonal structures, or manipulated by large and impersonal things like 'Society' or 'Historical Forces'. Lots of people then talked glibly about the power of The System.

One consequence of this approach was to suggest that anything as small-scale or as personal as group work would be quite irrelevant to any discussion of social change, let alone to any attempt to change The System.

Asking the 'right' questions

We have been very insistent that asking the right questions is the first step to taking effective action. Asking the right questions is important, especially for those of us who work in organisations like schools, colleges and universities that produce good learning and good research. But it is also important for those who work in the so-called third sector, comprising community agencies, or in non-government organisations—lobby groups and the diverse and colourful array of modern social movements.

Working effectively in groups will help us work better with those young people, women, workers, Aborigines, people with disabilities or those experiencing personal or social distress. Working in groups can also be a powerful way of making social change happen.

Asking the right questions matters because we need to establish how group work can address fundamental issues of personal and structural change in ways which promote social or ethical concerns and enhance people's capacity to participate as citizens. However, we should make no assumptions about any kind of group work being good at supporting this sort of activity. A lot of group work has been good at helping therapeutise people, but not very good at helping to promote social change.

Likewise, we should make no assumptions about the normal tendencies of organisations being to promote participation, citizenship rights, democracy or agency. Many organisations talk a lot about values like 'citizenship', 'democracy' or 'participation', but are painfully unable to give effect to them in their own practices and cultures. For example, how often are young people encouraged and permitted to be involved in decisions taken in their families— particularly when these decisions affect them directly? Or how often are those many young adults who attend our secondary colleges invited by government bureaucracies or the boards of private schools to be involved in shaping or refining the curriculum they are being taught? How often do university students get involved in curriculum planning in their degree courses? Or how often are the people about to be made unemployed consulted, let alone invited to participate in a problem-solving approach to a company's commercial problems? How frequently are ordinary workers closely involved with management in redesigning new work processes, routinely given budgetary details and involved in shaping the corporate culture?

Group work and social change

Can working with groups help to achieve social change? We believe it can do so. It is through working in groups that we make history. Through group activity we can organise to press governments for better health care or safer roads. By working with groups we can organise to deliver meals and other services to people who need them in their own homes, offer support to people with disabilities, or provide assistance to low-income people. Working in groups enables us to call for large-scale changes to the way we plunder the resources of the Earth or simply waste them in ways that are unsustainable. Working with groups can help a small community meet some need it has by organising its own resources better or get some new resources into that community. It can also be fundamental to a national struggle for liberation from oppression, exploitation and the exercise of power by unrepresentative elites (Briscoe & Thomas 1977). But let's start small.

Working with groups in the community

Social movements typically involve large struggles, involving significant numbers of people who want to change some basic feature of their social world. At a far less obvious level, there are the daily efforts of people working together who are concerned about issues or problems in their own neighbourhood or locality.

Community work

Community work and *community development* are two phrases used to refer to a range of political and professional activity (Briscoe & Thomas 1977). We do not want to get into debates about what differences—if any—there are between *community work* and *community development* and so refer simply to community work.

Community work is done in many different contexts (Kelly & Sewell 1989; Thorpe & Petruchenia 1992). It rests on a number of different philosophical positions (Plant 1974) and gives rise to a variety of practices which usually relate to promoting social justice or addressing some people's experience of oppression, exploitation or lack of access to resources (Rothman 1979; Thorpe & Petruchenia 1992). Most recently, Kenny (1994) has argued for its inclusion within a broader theory of social movements.

Community work

Central to community work is the idea that many people experience a lack of agency in their neighbourhood. They feel powerless and/or unable to shape their own future, or to plan or to manage their own lives. Community development involves people working together to overcome collective experiences of disempowerment. It is a style of social action predicated on the ideas of cooperation and solidarity rather than those of competition and individualism that are in favour among sections of Australian business and government in the 1990s.

- Community work can involve the employment of paid workers and professionals.
- It can involve developing networks.
- It can use groups as part of the techniques of empowerment.
- Much community work is not necessarily about 'building community' so much as it is about empowering specific groups and helping them to achieve agency.

Community work is usually done at a local level. A local primary school wants a new toilet block. Residents want a welfare program to help a group of elderly Australians. Sometimes this concern leads groups of people to wage campaigns in an effort to prevent the closure of a local swimming pool or the destruction of a local park—done in the name of development, budget cuts or to assist the tourist trade. Sometimes such action may be designed to prevent damage to the neighbourhood by the erection of mobile phone towers or to prevent possible ill-health effects from the construction of a high-power electricity line.

Social movements and working with groups

Perhaps most people can 'see' how groups are good for small-scale neighbourhood activity like establishing a créche for local toddlers, but what about the large-scale changes referred to here? How could anything like the civil rights movement in America or the Solidarity campaigns in Poland after 1970 have anything to do with groups and working with groups?

There are many examples of where this happened. We could begin by looking at the work of the National Association for the Advancement of Coloured People (NAACP) in winning basic rights for African Americans in the 1950s and 1960s. Beginning in 1954–55 in Montgomery, Alabama, a small network of local groups of the NAACP was galvanised by the presence of a new young preacher at the Dexter Church called Martin Luther King Jr. Through 1954 and 1955, a small number of African American women had been arrested for sitting in 'whites only' seats on the buses of Montgomery. The final catalyst was the arrest of Rosa Parks on 1 December 1955, which led to a small network of black women deciding enough was enough. Meeting in secret, they first drafted letters of protest, then decided to call for a boycott of the buses by all African Americans in Montgomery. The predominantly male black leaders of Montgomery were caught by surprise, but decided after several meetings to back the boycott. In a few days, a network of meetings and groups all across Montgomery was producing leaflets announcing the boycott, and had organised car pools to get African Americans to and from work. The whole exercise was led by a coalition of groups calling themselves the Montgomery Improvement Association, which, under King's leadership, organised the first of the increasingly successful exercises in civil disobedience that became the trademark of the black civil rights movement.

The point is a simple one: most of the successful campaigns for large-scale social or political change in the twentieth century have grown out of and depended on small groups of people (Eyerman & Jamison 1991). Often, at the end, there has been a mass movement of considerable complexity and scale, but at the heart of them all were small groups of people.

Social movements and social change

The twentieth century has seen the development of many social movements. However, few writers paid them much attention until the 1960s and 1970s.

Social movements

Social movements are . . . a collective expression of the belief that men and women are not subject to historical laws or material necessity, but that they can produce their own history through their cultural creations and social struggles, by fighting for control of those changes which will affect their collective and national life . . . (Touraine 1987, p. 35)

Group work and Australia's social movements in the 1990s

In Australia in the 1990s, there are many different kinds of social movements. Some of them currently use various group work styles. Some do not. All would benefit from a more systematic use of group work that is oriented towards promoting the goals and objectives of the movement.

Social movements typically involve large struggles involving large numbers of people who want to change some basic feature of their social world (Keane & Mier 1989). At a far less obvious level, there are daily struggles by people concerned about events in their own neighbourhood or locality.

Today in Australia, the various social movements exist as networks involving both small- and large-scale organisations and associations with activists, volunteers, core members and sympathisers, leaders and sometimes a structure of paid professional workers. There is no one single place or organisation where you will find these social movements—they are all over the place. You will find them in particular organisations as well as in newsletters and magazines. Social movements are evident in campaigns and protests, as well as in lobbying of governments and press releases.

The Women's Movement

The Women's Movement has been active and alive and well since the late 1960s, when organisations like Women's Liberation and the Women's Electoral Lobby began. It is found today in organisations like women's refuges, women's health collectives or in Centres Against Sexual Assault. It also exists inside the major political parties and in magazines and journals like *Hecate, Signs* or *Australian Feminist Studies.* It has lobbied for major law reform as well as for changes in major institutions like the schools, political parties and churches on questions that affect women. Recently, the movement for the ordination of women has put some of the churches into a difficult position. Some of the activists of the Women's Movement run consciousness-raising (CR) groups for women. Lesbian groups also offer a variety of social and counselling support programs. In addition, there are assertiveness training courses and many training programs for women who want to develop personal skills, political skills, negotiation skills and organisational skills.

Gay and lesbian movements

These movements manifest themselves in magazines like *Outrage* or newspapers like the *Melbourne Star*, in organisations like the Gay Men's Health Collective or in big annual events like the annual Sydney Gay and Lesbian Mardi Gras. As social movements, the gay and lesbian movements offer advice on health and emotional issues for gays and lesbians. In most of Australia's major cities, on-site and telephone counselling and advice services are provided. These movements lobby for law reform and better relations between the law and the community through special liaison groups to mediate between the gay community and the police forces of the various states. Some activists run consciousness-raising groups for men and for parents. Some organise health, legal advice and counselling services that are geared to the special needs of gays and lesbians. Since the early 1980s, the gay community has devoted considerable time, resources and energy to programs around AIDS, encouraging safe sex practices and preventive health care programs.

Union movement

The union movement is the oldest of the modern social movements. It represents about 35 per cent of Australian workers and operates at both state and national levels. At the national level, the movement is represented by the Australian Council of Trade Unions (ACTU). At the state level, there are various Trades Hall Councils or Trades and Labour Councils with offices in all capital cities and most major provincial cities. Workers also relate to their own union, which has a main office with full-time paid officials who are usually elected by the membership. There is still also a link between the unions and the Australian Labor Party (ALP). The union movement provides a number of services to members, including the protection of wages, conditions, occupational and health and safety issues, superannuation benefits and consumer benefits. The movement also runs regular training groups for its members.

Peace Movement

The Peace Movement in Australia has its origins in special-purpose groups established to fight the introduction of conscription in 1916–17 and again in the 1960s. Today it also draws on anti-nuclear campaigns by groups like People for Nuclear Disarmament (PD). It also has strong links with churches and church groups like *Pax Christie,* or elements within the ALP, as well as environmental groups like Greenpeace and other community groups. The Peace Movement finds expression in newsletters and journals like *Peace Studies,* as well as in street demonstrations.

Green Movement

The Green (or environmental) Movement is a more recent phenomenon, emerging in the 1970s as scientists and researchers documented the problems of toxic materials and gases, global warming, the destruction of rainforests and the hole in the ozone layer. It can be found in the form of organisations like Greenpeace, the Australian Conservation Foundation, Environment Victoria, the Wilderness Society and the Gould League. The activities of the environmental movement are evident in magazines like *Australian Geographic*. Members stage rallies and protests about logging, gases and dams and lobby the media and governments. More recently, this movement has helped to establish political parties like the Greens.

Church and community movements

These are often the largest and best resourced of the social movements, with their base in particular churches and in central offices which handle policy on issues relating to social justice and Third World development work for churches like the Uniting Church. There are agencies like the Salvation Army and Brotherhood of St Laurence, or St Vincent de Paul that run welfare services, perform research and lobby for policy changes. There are also tens of thousands of community-based organisations. Most often, these are very small with a few paid employees and lots of volunteers. They print newsletters, provide services and run a variety of self-help groups, training workshops and annual meetings.

In each of these movements, people work with groups that include:

- consciousness-raising groups where people learn how to assert themselves and how to learn from their own and/or other people's experiences;
- skills-training groups that help demonstrate how to negotiate better working conditions and/or how to organise a campaign or to lobby governments;
- self-help groups that offer mutual support, consumer benefits and/or a variety of emotional and psychological support;
- social action groups, through which the movement often tries to recruit new members, lobby governments to do things like set up a new school or stop something like logging.

How to work with groups in a social movement

There are not many essential major differences between social movements and community work. Both frequently involve the employment of paid workers and professionals; both involve developing networks; both use groups as one of their empowerment techniques. Social movements cover a lot of territory and involve large numbers of people. On the other hand, as we saw, community work is usually done on a smaller scale.

Group work can be an important part of community development and social movements. We are not, however, equating social movements with group work. Rather, we suggest that one part of the history of social movements and community development work is working with groups. Our role here is to suggest how groups and group work can play a valuable part in both social movements and community development.

We suggest that the earlier hints on good group practices in the community apply with the same force and have the same value when working with groups in any social movement setting.

Working with groups in the community and in social movements

Community work is based on the idea that people who are most affected by a particular problem are the people who are best able to articulate their experiences and then define and implement the solutions—hence the claim that among the core values of community work are self-management, empowerment, cooperation and sharing.

Three basic values for working with community groups and social movements

1 *Self-management*—Community work stresses the importance of face-to-face interactions, often in small groups or in networks of people working together. Most community work rests on faith in the capacity and the skills of 'ordinary' people to provide leadership, to work together, to overcome difficulties—including the problems raised when working with other people—and to develop organisational and political skills.

   Self-management refers to the belief and the expectation that various styles of democratic and inclusive decision-making generally work better in the long run than more elitist and authoritarian styles of organising people. This recognises that democratic styles of decision-making might seem to take longer, but that they produce better outcomes in the long run. (It is waiting for that 'long run' that can try people's patience occasionally!)

2 *Promoting people's agency*—This refers to people managing their own affairs and to the achievement over time of a growing sense of confidence and competence when making the decisions that affect them most directly.

Promoting agency refers both to a process and an objective. Promoting people's agency is a process where people get the confidence and develop the skills to make decisions. It also shares an objective with community work—that people come to be empowered. Promoting agency is not without its difficulties, because it often raises issues relating to the power of professionals and the role of professionals in community settings. Promoting people's agency can cause considerable anxiety and difficulty if groups pursue empowerment strategies in ways that upset professionals, or start to make decisions and judgments that certain professionals do not agree with.

3 *Cooperation*—Cooperation has for a long time been of central value in community work (Emery & Emery 1974). It represents a belief that in collective processes there is strength and wisdom greater and more worthwhile than that found in decisions made by one or two people, especially when those decisions affect many other people. Making collective action work means relying on people being tolerant, being prepared to compromise and being willing to see the value of collective decision-making—in other words, being cooperative. The value of cooperation often stands against notions of individualism, competition and hierarchy. Alongside faith in cooperation is the claim that basic to community work is the importance of groups sharing their problems and experiences (see Vatano 1972; Adams 1990, pp. 17–18).

Thinking about community work: Use your COMPASS

One recent way of thinking about community work and preparing to do it is the COMPASS model developed by Kelly and Sewell (1989). The COMPASS model is not a magic wand to solve all the problems that continually erupt. The value of the COMPASS is that it offers a series of checklist elements to think about as you get into the process.

It is especially good at raising basic ethical issues for anyone involved in working with groups and who wants to see some kind of social change take place. The COMPASS model has four points. It raises a series of questions for a community worker on the two dimensions: the in/out dimension, and the our/the people's interests dimension.

Figure 8.1 The COMPASS checklist

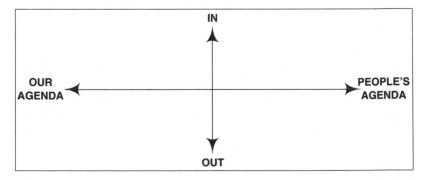

The COMPASS model raises questions like how much trust there is in the group and whose interests are going to take precedence when it comes to the point when conflicting interests erupt.

Becoming an 'insider'

The *in/out dimension* raises questions about the degree to which the community worker has developed a relationship of trust with his or her community. A community worker is initially often an outsider, who typically comes from another neighbourhood or suburb. He or she is often university trained in the social sciences and has human service work skills. Frequently the community worker comes into the community setting like a migrant, speaking a 'foreign' language, using words like 'heuristic' or 'dysfunctional families' or 'value base'. Furthermore, he or she may not know very much about the community, and may have little or no rapport with the local people at the start. The in/out dimensions raises the challenge of whether the worker will stay an 'outsider' or become an 'insider'.

Ideally the community worker needs to become at one with the people in the community he or she is working with, and be able to listen to them, to learn from them, to hear what they say. This requires considerable patience and skill. It is apparent that some community workers never move from their outsider status. For others, it is a struggle to become an insider. It is sometimes hard to not always refer to our own biography, to stop always using our own ways of thinking, to modify our language, to reflect on our pretensions, to re-think our training and to think critically about the prejudices it confers upon us. To stop being an 'outsider' and to become an 'insider' means a radical change in our own identity.

It is unlikely that we will be able to learn how to make this transition in a university or TAFE college—in fact, that privileged position is often what *makes* us an outsider. Becoming an insider begins by going into the local neighbourhood or community and it means working in the community to learn how to become an 'insider'.

Whose community?

The other axis (the *our agenda /people's agenda* dimension) raises the question of whose interests will shape the community work project, as well as the related question of whose ideas, expectations and values are central to a community development project. Should it be those of the professional or of 'the community'?

The first difficulty may be that the way the community worker sees the problem could be very different from the people's perceptions. There is no reason to believe that, because someone is the community worker, they have a better grasp of the actual problems and/or solutions. Indeed in this 'Century of Professions' (Perkins 1991), there is abundant evidence of the misery and distress caused by professionals who insist that their definition of the problems and solutions must dominate at the expense of other definitions and resolutions.

The second difficulty is that, among the members of the community, there may be no consensus about what the best solution is. If community work is defined as empowering the people of a community, then to impose a professional agenda is to distort the process and possibly impose distress upon the people of a community. To ask questions about whose agenda will be used (the people's or 'ours') is to raise our own (the professional's) consciousness about the ability of people to achieve their own agency. Will 'they' suffer the fate of having their problems replaced with the professional's definition of them and thus be further disempowered?

Talking about values like 'cooperation', 'tolerance' and 'democratic participation' is highly idealistic. As anyone who has actually worked in the community—or who has worked in social movements—knows, there is often a large gap between these fine principles and rhetoric and the often bitter and ugly behaviours that can erupt in these processes.

For example, remember that the idea of community as a principle is based on the practise of 'including' some people and 'excluding' others. Doing community work can lead to bitter fights over who is 'in' and who is 'out', or about whose political strategy will work best. There is also scope for conflict and difficulty in community work in the relationships between the paid professional workers and people in the community. Doing effective group work in community work projects calls for a considerable amount of sensitivity, patience and negotiating skills by the group facilitator and by all members of a group so as to make cooperation, tolerance and empowerment happen.

The role of group work in social change

Working in groups has an intense and immediate face-to-face quality. This makes it hard to write about and far better and 'easier' to learn by actually doing 'it'. But there are some useful bits of practice wisdom to be drawn on.

Hints for working with groups in social movements and the community

First—and without getting too prescriptive about it—there is often a sense of a 'life cycle' at work in many groups and it is useful to anticipate how this might work and be made to work to the advantage of the group.

Beginning phase

Groups can come together at the initiative of one or more people. The early success of these groups often depends on the degree of urgency and commitment that members bring to the group. It helps if such groups get a push and if the group has people in it who have a lot of energy, and who are committed, available and prepared to stay around. There is often a strong political or intellectual commitment to a cause, or a concern that something is wrong that needs to be put right. The initiator may decide to 'test the water' to see whether other people share his or her particular concerns or passions.

The beginning phase is usually about establishing the first relationships between members of the group. It is also about clarifying the purposes and goals of the group and working out whether there are any commonalities between members and what the emerging collective identity of the group is. In this phase, people may ask themselves questions like: Is this the group for me? What can I offer this group? Is there a fit between what I want to achieve and what this group seems to be setting out to achieve? Will I be able to get on with the people in this group?

This beginning phase requires people to work out how much the group is going to allow people to be themselves within it. It involves establishing how the group is going to work, what it will achieve, how much members are prepared to 'invest' in the group, and how much they want to reveal of themselves to other group members.

The role of the group worker/facilitator here may be to identify leaders or coordinators; recruit members to the group; establish some norms about decision-making and how much delegation needs to be undertaken, that is, who does what and how much democratic participation is to be the norm.

Clarifying issues of power and control

It does not take much time for issues of power, accountability and decision-making processes to emerge. People want to know who is going to play a leadership or coordinating role and how the group's decisions will be made. Sometimes some or all of the group's members try to define and formalise proceedings by developing rules and conventions about who gets the power, who the leader/s will be and how decisions will be taken. We have already explored this stage, which is referred to as the 'storming' phase. In other groups, especially those with a strong collective urge to get something done, such events may not occur.

At this point, there may be a number of power plays at work—or some more subtle processes involving contests for leadership and other competitive behaviours. This may take place amidst discussions about decision-making procedures and who is going to be responsible. These processes involve developing the norms and rules of the group, the leadership structure and how power is going to be distributed in the group. People may have certain interests to defend; they may have people and friendships to reward, old enemies to pay back, ideological battles to wage. So this process may be fraught with complexity and difficulty.

It is a mistake to assume that this process can always be successful or pain free. This is especially so in the 1990s, when issues of gender, ethnicity or age can be difficult to deal with in groups. Gender issues are frequently raised. Questions may be asked about how men and women talk to and relate to each other in the group. Women may be concerned about masculine ways of making decisions or about the way men tend to hog space, resources and time, while some men may feel diffident about what they see as being 'politically incorrect' or insensitive. Relations between black and white Australians can be similarly fraught, as can relationships between younger and older people.

There are also many other tensions that can surface in a group. These can include simple personality clashes—some people just do not get on with certain others, while some people have trouble handling disagreements. The skills and patience of any group facilitator will be tested, not to mention the equanimity of the other group members!

The group worker's role

The group worker's role may involve:

- encouraging the evolution of democratic procedure, or as much as the group wants;
- ensuring that any expertise the group worker possesses can be made available to the group in ways that assist it to achieve its goals;
- helping the group to manage political processes, while avoiding any problems like tendencies to maunder or bully, and ensuring that some people do not take over the group;
- trying to ensure that the leadership is representative of the wider group;
- ensuring that what people want to happen actually gets done.

In particular, the group facilitator should move early to do four things:

1 Establish at the beginning a set of boundaries for the group facilitator rather than assume that the group facilitator must or should play a central role in the group.
2 Determine that he or she will not decide the focus of the group, the pace of its activities or the goals of the group. Like any other member of the group, he or she may contribute ideas, suggestions for action or volunteer to do things.
3 Try to establish a democratic and equal relationship with the members of the group in terms of power and skills.
4 Try to act as a consultant rather than as an authoritative supervisor or leader. (Unell 1987, pp. 6–7)

There are some useful things anyone playing a facilitator role should try to do:

- Establish an agreement about aims and objectives for the group.
- Create a suitable organisational framework for the group, like length of meeting time, and agendas for each session.
- Help group members form a plan of action.
- Help the members of the group share the work.
- Help the group grasp and 'record' the results of its action.
- Assist the group to evaluate and adopt new or revised objectives in the light of the evaluation.

Decisions for the group to make

Key decisions need to be taken early and reviewed concerning the degree of formality in running the group.

- Will there, for example, be formal meetings with agendas and formal conclusions, with reviews and summaries of the group process?
- Will minutes or notes of the group process be kept, typed or copied and circulated?
- How will members be kept accountable for tasks they agree to undertake?
- Will there be formal processes for chairing and debating or determining maximum periods for which a member may speak?
- Will meetings be advertised?
- Will there be set times for beginning and ending the meetings?

- How will prospective members be dealt with?

Remember that one possible outcome is for the group to become entirely self-managing and for the group facilitator or leader to withdraw (Twelvetrees 1982, p. 39).

Addressing problems in groups

When the major process and leadership issues have been resolved, the group may be able to get on with its basic task or project. Hopefully, as time goes by, there is greater clarity about the purpose of the group and about its tactics and strategies. Sometimes conflict is not about the purpose of the group, but about people feeling left out and/or undervalued.

Relationships become stronger as trust between members increases. This, however, does not always happen—especially if there is a lot of stress and frustration. This may occur, for example, in the course of an active campaign such as that involved in the management of a strike or boycott, or in a major community campaign. Anger, anxiety and conflict can be part of the relationship-building process; such emotions can bind and strengthen some relationships, while destroying and weakening others. Conflict is a likely and normal aspect of any group process. Some groups thrive on conflict, but for others it can be extremely disruptive and unhelpful.

There are also endemic dangers in groups. Some people talk too much, while other people say little or nothing and some simply stop attending. Some people become the butt of the group's bad jokes. It is easy for one person to find or have given to them the role of scapegoat, to be blamed by the rest of the group for all the tensions and disappointments the group is experiencing. The other danger is that some people will drop out, fall into silence and/or become resentful.

Group facilitators and the group generally need to deal with disruptive, angry, assertive or violent members by:

- remembering that any disruption to a group may not only be the responsibility of the person who is doing it;
- realising that they can help the group get on with things by asking why they are seeking attention or exercising power in such a way;
- allowing the anger, frustration or conflict to have expression, rather than trying to deny it.

Acknowledging anger and conflict in the group allows you to work with it in constructive ways. People do get upset or annoyed at others who talk too much or who are loud or abusive. The best response may be to turn the group's attention (for an agreed amount of time) to address and review the situation with everyone present. Alternatively, it may be better to take a break and to spend some time with the person or people who are feeling upset and review the situation outside the group. When things are getting difficult, *call a break*!

Sometimes people need a chance to talk things over outside the group setting. Sometimes it is best to introduce a new activity or move the agenda along. It may also be appropriate for some people in the group to be counselled out of the group, rather than risk destroying the process for the other members.

Working together phase

As progress begins to be experienced by the group, there is usually considerable evidence of cohesion, and group members may start to increase their participation. People tend to joke and relax more, as well as show an increased willingness to share information with other people in the group. On the other hand, where there is evidence of conflict between people in the group, there is usually little evidence of a willingness to agree to disagree. In this phase we see the full value of working with groups.

Termination phase

Because many community interventions that use groups keep on keeping on, as they move to create committees to run a new centre or link up with some larger national or international movement, there may not always be a normal termination phase. However if the group does come to an end, this phase is described in Chapter 5.

Conclusion: Groups promote effective social change

1 Groups give people an opportunity to share experiences, develop and pursue common aims, learn from each other and learn how to effectively support each other.

2 Groups provide the chance to sort out relationship issues or political differences as well as develop and try out new skills.
3 Groups are useful because they help to reduce the feeling of being a powerless person working 'alone', by increasing opportunities to work with like-minded people.
4 Groups can be powerful sources of social change and help members to challenge sexual, racial or any other stereotypes, provide new role models, or provide new resources to overcome social exploitation or political oppression.
5 Groups can play a major role in developing new forms of political and social movement.
6 Groups can help people connect their own personal identity with larger social movements. For instance, groups can help establish the connection between being a feminist and a woman in the day-to-day business of working or being part of a family (see Toseland & Rivas 1984, pp. 8–9).

Review questions

1 Can you see an issue that you would like to address through social action?
2 What would your starting point be?
3 How you would plan to mobilise a group of people to take that action?

Glossary

Agency is the capacity of people to act and to plan in association with others to achieve their goals.

Altruism is self-sacrificing social action where an individual puts others' interests ahead of their own.

Child-saving was a nineteenth century social movement addressing social problems related to young people. Child-savers established child care institutions and kindergartens and tried to 'save children' from neglect and exploitation.

Community development refers to forms of action that draws on and organises the energies of local people and that are developed at a local level to solve local problems.

Conscientisation is a process of learning (developed by Paulo Friere) that involves groups of people renaming the world in ways that lead them to discover their capacity to act or to resist unfair or unjust treatment.

Consciousness-raising (CR) is a form of group learning that helps people to reflect on their life experiences. It can show people that certain events or conditions like poverty, unemployment or domestic violence, have more to do with socioeconomic and political arrangements than with the alleged deficiencies of a person.

Experiential learning is learning through doing.

Facilitation is a style of group work which encourages and promotes formative group development through very democratic styles of group work.

Forming is the first stage in the life cycle of groups, where members are concerned with getting to know each other as they establish the group's tasks.

Identity refers to how we see and experience ourselves and others in terms of gender, age, skin colour, occupation, religion, etc. We usually have a number of identities that change and sometimes even conflict with each other.

Leader style The leader leads rather than facilitates, relying on their authority to make decisions for the group.

Leadership style refers to the ways group leaders rely either on *facilitation* or the *leader style*.

Life cycle of group development This is a classic model that identifies five stages of group development: *forming, storming, norming, performing* and *mourning*. Stage five can also be a reforming stage.

Maundering is a form of poor group work facilitation characterised by 'idle incoherent rambling' talk: a lack of focus and purpose that interferes with and which even destroys positive group work.

Mourning is the final stage in the classic life-cycle model of groups when it is acknowledged that the group will soon end and when members may need support in disengaging from the group.

Normalism is a belief system like sexism or racism that uses differences— like physical appearance or behaviours—to mark off those who do not fit within the average range.

Norming is the third stage in the classic group life-cycle model. This stage is said to be characterised by a sense of 'togetherness' as group cohesion emerges.

Organisational group work uses groups and group work techniques in organisations to achieve certain objectives.

Performing is the fourth stage in the classic life-cycle model when members often demonstrate a high level of commitment to the group.

Philanthropists were/are people with high status, high incomes and a lot of moral concern about how others live, who work for the good of others without financial reward.

Professional, professionalism are terms used to claim status, authority and prestige for an occupation. To say you are professional is to claim a certain unique training, expert knowledge base and a superior ethical approach.

Racism is a belief system which insists that certain group characteristics like skin colour define all members of a cultural group.

Reciprocal perspective in group work refers to the development of mutual aid systems where people identify common issues and collectively develop solutions.

Remedial perspective describes group work in which experts work towards remedying distress, poverty or other problems. Experts working with this perspective use groups to help fix people's problems.

Sexism is a belief system which holds that there are biological differences between males and females and which results in the discriminating treatment of people on the basis of their gender.

Social control group work relies on the assumption that there are socially approved right and wrong ways to think and behave. It uses group techniques to help those identified as deviant or problematic to behave or think 'correctly' by re-educating or re-socialising people into 'appropriate' roles or ways of thinking.

Social goals perspective is a progressive political exercise directed towards promoting self-determination and social change.

Social roles are said to be scripts produced by 'society' that prescribe how a 'student' or a 'wife' is expected to behave, think or feel.

Storming according to the life-cycle model is the second phase in a group's development, characterised by conflict and struggle between members over who holds the power.

Structural functionalism is a theory of society which holds that there is a whole system (called 'society') based on a collective moral consensus and a form of social order based on everyone having a socially approved role. This order depends on the system's capacity to socialise new members effectively into a variety of social roles.

Structured experiences are activities designed to promote learning experiences for participants.

Therapeutic group work is intended to 'cure' problems like depression, anxiety or alcoholism. Its success also relies on the sharing of information and experiences.

Bibliography

Abberley, P. 1987 'The concept of Oppression and the Development of a Social Theory of Disability' *Disability, Handicap and Society* vol. 2, no. 1, pp. 37–56

Abel, K. 1979 'Toynbee Hall, 1884–1914' *Social Service Review* vol. 53, no. 4, December, pp. 606–29

Adams, R. 1990 *Self Help, Social Work and Empowerment* BASW/Macmillan, London

Argyris, C. 1990 *Overcoming Organisational Defences* Allyn and Bacon, Boston

Argyris, C. and Schon, D.A. 1978 *Organisational Learning* Addison Wesley, Reading, Mass.

Aries, P. 1969 *Centuries of Childhood: A Social History of Family Life* Knopf, New York

Aronowitz S. 1988 'Post-Modernism and Politics' *Universal Abandon? The Politics of Post-Modernism* ed. A. Ross, University of Minnesota Press, Minneapolis

Australian National Advisory Committee for UNESCO 1972 *A Basis for Youth Work in Australia* AGPS, Canberra

Bach, G.R. 1954 *Intensive Group Psychotherapy* Ronald Press, New York

Badger, C. 1979 *A History of Adult Education in Victoria* Cheshire, Melbourne

Baker, J. 1987 *Groupwork* Heineman, London

Bales, R. 1950 *Interaction Process Analysis: A Method for the Study of Small Groups* Addison-Wesley, Reading

Barcan, A. 1980 *A History of Australian Education* Oxford University Press, Melbourne

Beck, U., Giddens, A. & Scott, S. 1994 *Reflexive Modernization: Politics, Tradition and Aesthetics in the Modern Social Order* Polity Press, Oxford

Bertcher, H.J. 1979 *Group Participation: Techniques for Leaders and Members* Sage, Beverly Hills

Blumberg, A. & Golembiewski, R. 1976 *Learning and Change in Groups* Penguin, Harmondsworth

Boud, D., Cohen R. & Walker, D. (eds) 1993 *Using Experience for Learning* The Society for Research into Higher Education & Open University Press, Milton Keynes

Boud, D., Keogh, R. & Walker, D. (eds) 1985 *Reflection: Turning Experience into Learning* Routledge & Kegan Paul, London

Boy Scout Association 1959 *The Policy, Organisation and Rules of the Boy Scout Association* Boy Scout Association, London

Briscoe, C. & Thomas, D. (eds) 1977 *Community Work: Learning and Supervision* George Allen & Unwin, London

Brown L. 1991 *Groups for Growth and Change* Longman, New York

Button, L. 1972 *Discovery and Experience* Oxford, London

——1974 *Developmental Groupwork with Adolescents* University of London Press, London

——1982a *Group Tutoring for the Form Teachers: 1 Lower Secondary School* Hodder & Stoughton, London

——1982b *Group Tutoring for the Form Teachers: 2 Upper Secondary School; A developmental model* Hodder & Stoughton, London

Canguilhem, G. 1993 *From the Normal to the Pathological* Spectrum Books, New York

Carkhuff, R. 1969 *Helping and Human Relations* (vols 1–2) Holt, Rinehart & Winston, New York

Cartwright, D. & Zander, A. 1960 *Group Dynamics: Research and Theory* Tavistock, Illinois

Connell, R.W. 1995 *Masculinities* Allen & Unwin, Sydney

Connell, W.F. 1964 *Youth Service and Youth Leadership* Australian Frontier, Canberra

——1980 *A History of Education in the Twentieth Century World*, Curriculum Development Centre, Canberra

Cooper, T. & White, R. 1994 'Models of Youth Work Intervention' *Youth Studies Australia* Summer, pp. 13–17

Corbett, J. 1994 'So Who Wants to be Normal?' *Disability, Handicap and Society* vol. 6, no. 3, pp. 23–34

Crawley, J. 1978 'The Life Cycle of the Group' *Small Groups Newsletter* vol. 1, no. 2, pp. 39–44

Davidson, G. 1981 *The Rise and Fall of Marvellous Melbourne*, Melbourne University Press

Degon, M. 1988 *Jane Addams and the Men at the Chicago School: 1892–1918* Transaction Books, New Brunswick

Douglas, T. 1976 *Groupwork Practice* Tavistock, London

——1978 *Basic Groupwork* Tavistock, London

——1979 *Groupwork Processes in Social Work* Wiley, Chichester

——1983 *Groups* Tavistock, London

Duke, C & Sommerlad, E. 1981 'Experimental Small Group Learning and the Human Relations Movement' *Canberra Papers in Continuing Education* ed. N. Haines, ANU, Canberra

Dunnette, M. 1972 'Research Needs of the Future in Industrial Organisations' *Personal Psychology* vol. 23, pp. 31–40

Emery, F.E. & Emery, M. 1974 *Participative Design, Work and Community Life* Occasional Paper in Continuing Education, Paper No. 4, Centre for Continuing Education, ANU, Canberra

Epstein, I. 1970 'Professional Role Orientation and Conflict Strategies' *Social Work* vol. 15, no. 4, October, pp. 87–92

Erikson, E. 1963 *Childhood and Society* 2nd edn, Norton, New York

Evans, J. 1994 *Experiential Learning for All* Cassell Education, London

Eyerman, R. & Jamison, A. 1991 *Social Movements: A Cognitive Account* Polity Press, Cambridge

Facey, A.B. 1985 *A Fortunate Life* Fremantle Arts Centre Press, Perth

Foucault, M. 1979 *Discipline and Punish* Penguin, Harmondsworth

Freire, P. 1974 *Education for Critical Consciousness* Sheed and Ward, London

Fryer, D. 1995 'Benefit Agency? Labour Market Disadvantage, Deprivation and Mental Health' *The Psychologist* vol. 78, June, pp. 51–56

Fulcher, G. 1989 *Disabling Policies* Palmer Press, London

Gale, J.A. 1974 *Group Work in Schools* McGraw-Hill Book Co., Sydney

Gardiner, H. 1987 *Multiple Intelligences* Basic Books, New York

Giddens, A. 1991 *Modernity and Self Identity* Polity Press, Cambridge

Hamilton-Smith, E. & Brownell, D. 1973 *Youth Workers and Their Education* YWA, Melbourne

Heaney, S. 1980 *Preoccupations* Faber & Faber, London

Hirst, J.B. 1973 *Adelaide and the Country 1870–1917* Melbourne University Press

Homans, G.C. 1950 *The Human Group* Harcourt, New York

——1961 *Social Behaviour: Its Elementary Forms* Harcourt Brace Jovanovich, New York

Howe, M. 1977 'Trailing and Work: Inservice Training for Psychologists in State Education Departments' *Psychology in Australia* ed. M. Nixon & R. Taft, Pergamon Press, Sydney

Hunter, I. 1994 *Rethinking the School* Allen & Unwin, Sydney

Husock, H. 1993 'Bringing Back the Settlement House' *Public Welfare* vol. 45, no. 2, pp. 16–25

Illich, I. 1983 *Disabling Professions* Marion Boyar, London

Jaggs, D. 1986 *Neglected and Criminal: Foundations of Child Welfare in Victoria* Centre for Youth and Community Studies, Phillip Institute of Technology, Coburg

Jenner, L. 1995 Disability, Identity and Friendship: The Struggle to Affirm What Others Deny, Unpublished MA Minor Thesis, RMIT, Melbourne

Johnson, D. & Johnson, F. 1982 *Joining Together: Group Theory and Group Skills*, Prentice-Hall, Englewoods Cliffs

——1987 *Joining Together: Group Theory and Group Skills* Prentice-Hall, Englewoods Cliffs

Jones, B. 1982 *Sleepers, Wake!* Oxford University Press, Melbourne

Keane, J. & Mier, P. (eds-trans) 1989 *Alberto Meluuci, Nomads of the Present: Social Movements and Individual Needs in Contemporary Society* Hutchinson Radius, London

Kelly, A. & Sewell, S. 1989 *With Heads, Hearts and Hands, Dimensions of Community Building* Boolarong Press, Brisbane

Kennedy, R. (ed.) 1989 *Australian Welfare: Critical Sociology* Macmillan, Melbourne

Kenny, S. 1995 *Developing Communities for the Future: Community Development in Australia* Nelson, Melbourne

Kett, J.F. 1977 *Rites of Passage: Adolescence in America. 1970 to the Present* Basic Books, New York

Klein, J. 1963 *Working With Groups: The Social Psychology of Discussions and Decisions* Hutchinson University Library, London

——1966 *Working with Groups* Hutchinson, London

Landells, W. 1983 *The Try Society* Try Society, Melbourne

Langley, G. 1992 *A Decade of Dissent: Vietnam and the Conflict on the Australian Home Front* Allen & Unwin, Sydney

Leonard, P. 1975 'A Paradigm for Radical Practice' *Radical Social Work* ed. R. Bailey & M. Brake, Edward Arnold, London

Levine, M. & Levina, A. 1992 *Helping Children: A Social History* Oxford University Press, New York

Lewin, K. 1943 'Psychology and the Process of Group Living' *Journal of Social Psychology* vol. 17, pp. 113–31

——1947 'Group Decisions and Social Change' *Readings in Social Psychology* ed. T. Newcombe & E.L. Hartley, Holt, Rinehart & Winston, New York

——1951 *Field Theory in Social Science* Harper, New York

Lewis, J. 1987 'So Much Grit in the Hub of the Educational Machine' in *Mother State and Her Little Ones* ed. B. Bessant, Centre for Youth and Community Studies, Melbourne

Liffman, M. 1978 *Power for the Poor: The Family Centre Project—An Experiment in Self-Help*, Allen & Unwin, Sydney

McGhee, J. & Fryer, D. 1989 'Unemployment Income and the Family' *Social Behaviour* vol. 4, pp. 237–54

McGill, I. & Beatty, L. 1992 *Action Learning* Kogan Page, London

McLachlan, N. 1951 Larrikinism: An interpretation, Unpublished MA thesis, History Department, University of Melbourne

Massey, J.T. 1950 *The YMCA in Australia: A History* Cheshire, Melbourne

Mayo, E. 1933 *The Human Problem of an Industrial Civilisation* Macmillan, London

Milgram, S. 1979 *Obedience to Authority* Hutchinson, London

Mills, C. Wright 1970 *The Sociological Imagination* Penguin, Harmondsworth

Milson, F. 1973 *An Introduction to Groupwork Skill* Routledge & Kegan Paul, London

Morris, J. 1992 'Personal and Political: A Feminist Perspective on Researching Physical Disability' *Disability, Handicap and Society* vol. 7, no. 2, pp. 13–28

Murray-Smith, S. & Dare, A.J. 1987 *The Tech: A Centenary History of the Royal Melbourne Institute of Technology* Hyland House, South Yarra

Nadel, G. 1957 *Australia's Colonial Culture* Melbourne University Press, Melbourne

Nixon, M. & Taft, R. (eds) 1977 *Psychology in Australia: Achievements and Prospects* Pergamon Press, Sydney

O'Connor, I., Wilson, J. & Setterlund, D. 1995 *Social Work and Welfare Practice* 2nd edn, Longman, Melbourne

O'Neill, W. 1977 'Teaching and Practice of Psychology in Australia' *Psychology in Australia: Achievements and Prospects* ed. M. Nixon & R. Taft, Pergamon Press, Sydney, pp. 2–23

Oakley, C. 1936 'Some Psychological Problem of a Depressed Area' *Human Factor* vol. 10, pp. 393–404

Onians, E. 1914 *The Men of Tomorrow* Lothian, Melbourne

Perkins, H. 1991 *The Rise of Professional Society* Routledge, London

Plant, R. 1974 *Community and Ideology: An Essay in Applied Social Philosophy* Routledge & Kegan Paul, London

Platt, A.M. 1984 *The Child Savers* 2nd edn, University of Chicage Press, Chicago

Ramsland, J. 1986 *Children of the Backlanes* University of NSW Press, Kensington

Roethlisberger, F. & Dickinson, W. 1939 *Management and the Worker* Harvard University Press, Cambridge

Rogers, C. 1965 *Encounter Groups* Penguin, Harmondsworth

——1969 'The Therapeutic Relationship: Recent Theory and Research' *Australian Journal of Psychology* vol. 17, pp. 95–108

Rose, N. 1989 *Governing the Soul* Routledge, London

Roszack, T. 1974 *The Making of a Counter Culture* Faber & Faber, London

Rothman, J. 1974 *Planning and Organising for Social Change* Columbia University Press, New York

——1979 'Three Models of Community Organisation Practice' *Strategies of Community Organisation* ed. F. Cox, J. Erelich, J. Rothman & J. Tropman, Peacock Press, Illinois

Rowse, T. 1978 *Australian Liberalism and National Character* Kibble Press, Malmsbury

Schon, D. 1983 *The Reflective Practitioner: How Professionals Think in Action* Basic Books, New York

Selleck, R. 1968 *The New Education* Pitman, London

Senge, P. 1990 *The Fifth Discipline: The Art and Practice of the Learning Organisation* Random House, Sydney

Sennett, R. 1993 *Authority* Faber & Faber, London

Shaw, M. 1971 *Group Dynamics: The Psychology of Small Group Behaviour* McGraw-Hill, New York

——1981 *Group Dynamics* 3rd edn, McGraw-Hill, New York

Sprott, W.J. 1958 *Human Groups* Penguin, Harmondsworth

Stanley-Hall, G. 1904 *Adolescence: Its Psychology and its Relations to Physiology, Anthropology, Sociology, Sex, Crime, Religion and Education* 2 vols, D. Appleton, New York

Stedman-Jones, G. 1969 *Outcast London* Penguin, Harmondsworth

Szirom, T. & Dyson, S. 1984 *Greater Expectations* YWCA, Melbourne

Szirom, T. & Spartels, D. 1995 *A Framework for Practice-based Training in Youth Work* SACSITB, Melbourne

Theobald, M. & Selleck, R.J. (eds) 1990 *Family, School and State in Australian History* Allen & Unwin, Sydney

Thorpe, R. & Petruchenia, J. (eds) 1992 *Community Work or Social Change: An Australian Perspective* 2nd edn, Routledge & Kegan Paul, London

Toseland, R. & Rivas, R. 1984 *An Introduction to Groupwork Practice*, Macmillan, New York

Touraine, A. 1974 *The Post-Industrial Society: Tomorrow's Social History: Classes, Conflict and Culture in the Programmed Society* Wildwood House, London
——1981 *The Voice and the Eye: An Analysis of Social Movements* Cambridge University Press, Cambridge
——1987 *Solidarity* Cambridge University Press, Cambridge
Trowbridge, R. 1995 Interview, December 1995
Truax, C.B. & Carkhuff, R. 1967 *Towards Effectiveness Counselling and Psychotherapy* Aldine, Chicago
Twelvetrees, A. 1982 *Community Work* BASW/Macmillan, London
Tyson, T. 1989 *Working with Groups* Macmillan, Melbourne
Unell, J. 1987 *Help for Self-Help: A Study of a Local Support Group* NCVO, London
van Krieken, R. 1991 *Children and the State* Allen & Unwin, Sydney
Vatano, A. 1972 'Power to the People—Self-help Groups' *Social Work* vol. 17, no. 4, pp. 7–15
Watson, H., Vallee, J. & Mulford, B. 1980 *Structured Experiences and Group Development* Curriculum Development Centre, Canberra
Weil, S.W. & McGill, I. (eds) 1989 *Making Sense of Experiential Learning* The Society for Research into Higher Education & Open University Press, Milton Keynes
Williams, A. 1991 *Forbidden Agendas: Strategic Action in Groups* Tavistock/ Routledge, London
Williams, E. 1972 'The Beginnings of the Australian University Extension Movement' *Melbourne Studies in Education*, pp. 185–210
Wills, G. 1995 'The Problem of Inequality' *Financial Review* 8 May
Wolfensberger, W. 1972 *The Principle of Normalization in Human Services* National Institute on Mental Retardation, Toronto
——1983 'Social Role Valorization: A Proposed New Term for the Principal of Normalization' *Mental Retardation* vol. 34, no. 2, pp. 57–71
Wrong, D. 1969 'The Oversocialized Conception of Man' *Introduction to Sociology: Readings* ed. P. Worsley, Penguin, Harmondsworth
Yeatman, A. 1992 *Bureaucrats, Technocrats, Femocrats: Essays on the Contemporary Australian State* Allen & Unwin, Sydney
Zastrow, C. 1989 *Social Work with Groups* Nelson Hall, Chicago

Index